How to Succeed

as a Parent

How to Succeed as a Parent

Steve Chalke

Hodder & Stoughton

LONDON SYDNEY AUCKLAND

First published in Great Britain in 1997
This new edition first published in 2003

10 9 8 7 6 5 4 3 2 1

British Library Cataloguing in Publication Data
A record for this book is available from the British Library

ISBN 0 340 86136 3

Typeset in Garamond by Avon DataSet Ltd, Bidford-on-Avon, Warwickshire

Printed and bound in Great Britain by
Clays Ltd, St Ives plc

The paper and board used in this paperback are natural recyclable products
made from wood grown in sustainable forests. The manufacturing processes
conform to the environmental regulations of the country of origin.

Hodder & Stoughton
A Division of Hodder Headline Ltd
338 Euston Road
London NW1 3BH
www.madaboutbooks.com

Contents

Acknowledgments

A big thank you to those who read and commented on the manuscript: Sarah and Neil Altman, Joe and Rachel Davis, Barbara Evwaraye, Richard and Sheilagh Eyre, Barry and Margaret Lock, Jerry Thomas, Liz and Steve Turner, and Derek and Dawn Underwood.

Thanks also to Judith Longman, Charles Nettleton and the whole team at Hodder, and to everyone at Parentalk and Oasis, especially Andrew Carruthers, Paul Hansford, Lorraine Ingham, Kristen Meadows, Charlotte Mungeam, Ivor Peters and Heather Underwood.

Most of all, a special thank you to my wife, Cornelia, and to our children – Emily, Daniel, Abigail and Joshua – through whose patience I am slowly learning what it means to be a parent.

Just for the Record

For most people, *becoming* a parent is relatively easy. Almost anyone can do it. You don't need a licence, formal qualifications, or *any* real knowledge at all about children in order to produce one.

It's *being* a parent that's the tough bit. At one and the same time it's the most wonderful privilege and daunting challenge of your life. You suddenly find yourself responsible for a helpless and impressionable infant who depends on you for absolutely everything. And it's your job not just to meet all their needs, but to spend the next eighteen or so years ensuring they get the best possible start in life. This 'small task' is one that'll stretch you more than anything you've ever attempted before . . . and probably more than anything you'll ever face in the future. But if you're willing to take it on and give it your best, it can also prove to be the most exciting, rewarding and fulfilling experience of your life!

Families aren't standard issue. They come in all shapes and sizes – not just the classic Hollywood version of mum, dad, two kids and a dog. There are models with one child and those with six – even those where all six were born together! There are those where the children, or some of them, have been adopted, and those where one or more is physically disabled or has a learning disability. And then, for all sorts of different reasons, there are those with just one parent – sometimes a mum, sometimes a dad. And sometimes there's a step-parent and stepchildren. But whatever your situation, this book is for you. Because it's about the basic principles and skills that every parent, regardless of their individual circumstances, needs in order not only to *survive* being a parent, but to *thrive* on the whole thrilling experience.

For the record, I want to get one or two things straight right from the start.

First, most of the best ideas contained in this book aren't original. They're second-hand. They're lessons I've learnt from people who've trodden the long road of learning about what it takes to be a parent before me. After all, as someone once said, 'Why learn from your own mistakes when you can learn from someone else's?' But nevertheless, everything you'll find in these pages is also the result of twenty years of personal experience.

Second, I realise that you might not agree with everything I've written here. In fact, I'm half expecting that you won't. One of my aims when I first thought about writing this book was simply to trigger thought and discussion, because I'm convinced that what we come to *believe* about being parents makes a huge difference to the way we *behave* as parents.

Third, this book doesn't contain any detailed instructions about what size of nappy to get for your baby, exactly what time to send your child to bed on school nights, or whether or not to let your teenager go clubbing. Instead, it sets out ten honest, practical, tried and tested tips to help you on your way to becoming the best parent you can be.

Lastly, I don't claim for a moment to know all there is to know about being a parent, and I'm definitely not the *perfect* dad. As the father of four children – two girls and two boys, currently aged twenty, eighteen, sixteen and fourteen – there's lots about being a parent that I've learnt the hard way as I've gone along. But the race isn't over yet, and I'm still learning. My 'L' plates are firmly attached.

So reading this book won't tell you how to become a *perfect* parent. The truth is, there's no such thing. But I do believe that you can be a *successful* parent. Because successful parents aren't ones who never make mistakes. They're ones who know and acknowledge their failings, but trust their own judgment, and constantly work hard at the whole daunting and challenging – but at the same time wonderfully exciting – task of giving it their best shot.

Tip One

Be Realistic

There's no such thing as a perfect parent

'My sister's expecting a baby, and I don't know if
I'm going to be an uncle or an aunt.'

Chuck Nevitt

Everything changes when a baby comes along

In the film *When Harry Met Sally*, Sally recalls how her friend
Alice used to complain that 'she and Gary never did it any
more'. They were both too exhausted. Their kids drained them
of every sexual impulse they'd once had. With no children to
get in the way, on the other hand, Sally boasted that she 'could
have sex on the kitchen floor' whenever she wanted, and never
have to worry about them walking in.

When Cornelia and I first got married, we could go for
romantic walks in the countryside and have evenings to
ourselves. We could lie in the bath for hours, stay up late, stay
out late, go to restaurants and the cinema, and plan cheap
holidays in term-time. In short, we had freedom . . . and, most
importantly of all, we had the energy to be able to use it.

If you're already a parent, like me, you can probably just
about remember a time like this, in the dim and distant past,
when you used to wake up every morning next to your partner,
when your sleep was uninterrupted, or when the loo seat hadn't
been piddled over every time you needed to use it.

And then, one day, everything changed. Your life was

3

WE'RE ABOUT TO HAVE A BABY, A STEEP LEARNING CURVE AND AN ENTIRELY DIFFERENT LIFESTYLE...

suddenly turned upside down. Nowadays, if a warm feeling engulfs you when you're half asleep in bed in the morning, it's because your sweet and beautiful toddler has climbed in with you and wet themselves again! Now you come to in the morning feeling unrested and uncomfortable, only to find yourself hanging half off the bed with your little son's foot in your back. Your partner, who *was* pushed out of bed, has taken refuge on the downstairs sofa. You deliberately bought a king-size bed just so you'd never have to fight for space or your share of the duvet, but now your little angel is lying horizontally across the pillows, fast asleep!

I remember walking into the hospital before my eldest child was born, with no real idea how much my life was about to be turned upside down. When I entered the ward, I was a carefree, married man in my mid-twenties. When I left, six hours later, I was a *father*. The transformation was total and immediate. Life would never be the same again. The buzz was incredible, but so was the burden of responsibility.

We live in an 'instant' age. We eat instant meals, drink instant coffee, use instant communication and get offered instant credit. So you'd think we'd be ready for the shock of an Instant Family. But we're not. Why? Because most of the 'instants' in our lives are designed to be 'labour-saving'. Children, on the other hand, have exactly the opposite effect: they don't *save* energy and effort, they *demand* it.

> **'The night you were born, I ceased being my father's boy and became my son's father. That night I began a new life.'**
>
> Henry Gregor Felson

Your child's early years are formative years

Being a parent is a wonderful experience, but it's also a huge responsibility. What we do today as parents has a fundamental impact on what our children become tomorrow. Andrew, a forty-year-old friend of mine, claims that he's still basically a 'prisoner of his childhood'. And he's not alone. Some people spend many years and vast amounts of money on therapy sessions, trying to sort out all their emotional problems related to the murky depths of their childhood years.

In the film *Parenthood*, Gil wants to give his children the loving, stable family environment he never had as a child. But he worries that he's not doing very well. When he's in a confident mood, he imagines his son, Kevin, graduating as the most outstanding university student in his year, and publicly thanking his dad for helping him become 'the happiest, most confident, most well-adjusted person in the world'. The speech is so moving, it brings tears to Gil's eyes. But when he feels he's failing to be the kind of dad he wants to be, Gil imagines Kevin becoming a psychopathic monster who ends up going on an orgy of violence. And it's all his fault, because he didn't get it right.

The truth is, for all the enjoyment – and it really is enjoyable – being a parent is also a massive responsibility. We have a huge influence on our children's lives. How they turn out has a great deal to do with what kind of parents we are. And since our kids will probably have kids of their own, our performance will also have a big impact on the next generation as well. Which means that if we get it right, we'll make the task of parenting much easier for our own children. All this is a huge burden for anyone to carry, and it can make some parents just throw up their hands in despair.

> **'I used to have 4 theories on child-rearing and no kids. Now I have 4 kids and no theories.'**
>
> Dr James Dobson

Kids don't come with an instruction manual

Before they become parents, most people have got it all sorted. They carefully observe the way other parents raise their kids, noting their mistakes. Couples smile at each other in a knowing sort of way. They know just how *not* to do things. *They'd* never do anything even remotely as shortsighted as the Joneses did. *They'd* never shout at, smack, spoil or bribe their children. *They'd* never sit them in front of the television just to shut them up. They'd always be in complete control.

To be honest, Cornelia and I were just the same before we got married and had kids of our own. We had standards and expectations, and we were sure we weren't going to be disappointed. *Our* kids would be polite, thoughtful and sweet-natured. They'd always say 'please' and 'thank you'. They'd never misbehave at table, throw food, pick their nose, or fight. It was all so straightforward.

Now I know that the only people who are certain how to

raise kids are those who've never had any. They've still got the kind of naïve, know-it-all 'expertise' that parents have had knocked out of them by experience. Before you have a child, you can afford to have Ten Commandments on how to raise a Happy Family. But by the time your first child is a year old, you've had to downgrade them to Ten Handy Hints, and within another year you've abandoned them altogether!

The truth is that none of the 'prepackaged' rules people come up with before they have children actually work. Before they have kids, every parent believes they can do a near-perfect job. But the moment they hold their new-born son or daughter in their arms, their confidence disappears and their theories evaporate. Perfection stops being a realistic goal and becomes a massive burden. In the space of just a few weeks or months, a new parent moves from seeing themselves as the Parenting Heavyweight Champion of the World to feeling totally outclassed and pinned against the ropes! Now it's just a matter of survival.

Cornelia and I didn't plan to have our first child when we did. In fact, having a baby was the last thing we had on our minds when we conceived her. And as she lay in my arms in the delivery room, I confess it was hard to make the very obvious connection between that moment of passionate intimacy and this squealing, squirming, wrinkled ball of pink flesh. A few minutes of fun . . . and *now* look! I was half hoping that the contractions would begin again and out would pop an A4 cellophane wrapper containing the instruction book, like the one you get with a new computer or video recorder. It might be badly translated from the original Japanese, but it's still worth having. In fact, in the case of a child, most parents would settle for *anything* – even if it was still in Japanese!

> **'To a young boy, the father is a giant from whose shoulders you can see forever.'**
>
> Perry Garfinkel

Families have shrunk in the wash

The Navajo Indians of North America still incorporate a kind of 'Marriage Race' into every wedding. As part of the ceremony, all the women in the village run around its boundaries with the new bride. The bride finishes this 'race' first, with her immediate family – her mother, aunts and sisters – close behind, and all the other women just behind them. But this isn't a tradition designed to make sure that all the women of the village get regular exercise. It's a powerful symbol of the way the Navajo recognise that every new couple needs ongoing support from the whole community.

There was a time in our culture when we wouldn't have needed to look for help or advice from experts and professionals outside the immediate family. Uncles, aunts, parents, grandparents and great-grandparents all lived in the same village. They were there to offer useful and relevant guidance, support and babysitting when you wanted it. But the 'family' has shrunk considerably in the last century. Fifty years ago, your mother lived in the same street. One hundred years ago, she lived in the same house. Now you're lucky if she even lives in the same town or county. Maybe you never had a mum and dad to learn your parenting skills from in the first place. Or maybe you're a single parent, on your own and 'on duty' twenty-four hours a day with no example to follow.

Smaller families have given us independence, but at what cost? As families and communities grow apart, people are becoming more than just independent. They're also becoming more isolated. Entire communities used to play a part in the raising of every child. Now the individual is often left to fend for themselves.

> **'The essential skill of parenting is making up answers. When an experienced father is driving down the road and his kid asks him how much a certain building weighs, he doesn't hesitate for a second. "Three thousand, four hundred and fifty-seven tons," he says.'**
>
> Pam Brown

Parenting can be a real *Mission Impossible*

The task ahead for a new parent today can seem virtually impossible. As they handed me my new-born baby, I could almost hear a voice inside my head saying: '*Good morning, Mr Chalke. The baby you're now looking at is yours. Your mission, should you decide to accept it, is to raise her until she's old enough to make her own decisions and take responsibility for her own life. As usual, should you or any of your team be captured, everyone else will deny all knowledge of this operation. This tape will self-destruct in five seconds.*'

And what makes this *Mission Impossible* particularly daunting is the total lack of real experience that a new parent has. At least Jim Phelps could rely on seasoned experts to help him get the job done. The team in the famous TV series never failed in its mission because everyone knew just what they were doing. New parents have no idea what they're doing, no guarantee that they're following the right tactics, and no certainty that it'll succeed. In short, they start their mission with no preparation, no rehearsal and no plan.

Normally, before we have to do anything important, we get the chance to prepare ourselves for it in advance. Exams, driving tests, playing the recorder in the school concert . . . whatever it is, we get to rehearse it over and over again first. For most couples, there's even a walk-through rehearsal the day before the wedding to ensure that all key players know where they're supposed to stand, what they're supposed to say, and when they're supposed to say it. But nothing can adequately prepare you to be a parent. No matter how ready you think you are beforehand, it's never enough, and the real thing will always take you by surprise.

> **'I was the same kind of father as I was a harpist. I played by ear.'**
>
> Harpo Marx

Parenting is mostly 'make it up as you go along'

Parenting Advice is now a boom industry. There are 'experts' and 'professionals' galore telling us exactly what we're doing wrong and how to correct it in the future. As a result, we have to cope not just with our children, but with the experts as well. Advice is constantly on offer from an overwhelming variety of places: books, magazines, TV, and no doubt from Internet Nannies as well.

If you're anything like me, this advice is sometimes intimidating. It often makes me feel even more guilty about messing things up than I did before. And my feelings of guilt and inadequacy are then reinforced by Hollywood pictures of healthy, happy, low-fat, low-cholesterol, all-singing, all-dancing, minty-fresh families, with perfect smiles and pure white teeth, calmly eating a balanced breakfast in a wonderfully clean and hygienic fully-fitted kitchen.

But the truth is that perfect happy families simply don't exist. Breakfast is always a war zone. If we fall for the lie that there's a happy family with no real problems just down the road, we're bound to end up demoralised when we don't live up to their standard. But behind the front door, these families have the same troubles, tensions, squabbles and dilemmas as everyone else. As they say, the grass may be greener 'over there', but it still needs mowing!

There's no magic fomula, $x+y=mc^2$, that'll solve all your parenting problems. There's not even any guarantee that what works with one child one day will work with the same child, or any other child, the next. Parenting is more like improvised music than maths. There are some very important broad principles, but most of it's a matter of individual flair and style.

THE MAIN INGREDIENTS FOR SUCCESSFUL PARENTING ARE THE DESIRE TO WORK AT IT AND A SENSE OF HUMOUR..

HEY, A CHILD COULD HAVE TOLD YOU THAT.

It doesn't matter how many books you've read on playing the violin, or how many concerts you've been to. It still takes months of patient, dedicated practice just to make a noise that doesn't sound like a strangled cat. It usually takes years to sound good. And you never stop learning. Parenting is the same. Whatever you've heard or read, you can't expect to get it all right from the start. Success is the result of making good decisions. Good decisions are the result of experience. And experience is the often painful result of learning from all your bad decisions. But however long you've been at it, you're still a learner and you'll still get frustrated with your own performance.

Parenting may be life's greatest adventure, but it's also life's greatest experiment. Being a mum or dad is trial and error: unbalanced, unplannable, unpredictable and chaotic. And even when you've been doing it for years, you still have to make most of it up as you go along. It's all about improvisation.

In fact, parenting makes playing the violin look like beginner's stuff. Because, unlike playing the violin, all of your rehearsing takes place on stage. You make your mistakes in full view of the critics and the rest of the world, who are often only too ready to tell you what you're doing wrong. And you can't start again from the beginning if you mess things up. The truth is that half the skill of parenting is trying to correct mistakes in mid-performance!

So even having lots of children doesn't qualify someone to give absolute, set-in-stone, tried and tested, Good Housekeeping Seal of Approval rules for success. Why? Because there just aren't any! Other parents can share what they've learnt from personal experience. Experts can outline the basic principles. But no one can give you failsafe, guaranteed-to-succeed rules for what to do in every situation. Every child, and therefore every relationship, is different.

'An alarm clock is an object used for waking up people who don't have kids.'

Anonymous

You can never be a PERFECT parent, but you can be a GREAT one

It's probably too late to say this, but if it's an easy life you're after, don't have children. Being a parent is, as a friend of mine puts it, an 'exhilarating trip'. In fact, it's 'the time of your life'. But it's also very demanding. So if you're after an easy life, buy a baby video instead. That way you can turn it off and put it away when you've had enough. Alternatively, plant rose bushes in your garden or build model railways in your attic. Whatever you do, use every available means of contraception! After all, even God had problems as a dad: just look how Adam and Eve turned out!

But if you're already a parent, don't panic. The fact that you're reading this book is a good sign. It proves that you want to be as great a parent as you possibly can be, and that's very important. It's the parents who won't listen or think they've got it all sewn up who're really in trouble.

Anyway, first the bad news: perfect parenting isn't just beyond *your* abilities, it's beyond *everyone's* abilities. Put simply, to be a perfect parent, you'd have to be a perfect person, and there aren't any of those anywhere in the world. We all make mistakes. Everyone does and says things that, with hindsight, they wish they hadn't.

Now the good news: though you'll never be a *perfect* parent, you *can* be a good parent. You can even be a *great* parent. The truth is, *most* parents who are willing to put in the time and effort, do a good job. But sadly, they still tend to torture themselves with guilt because they're worried they're doing something wrong. In fifteen years dealing with family problems – both personally as a father and professionally with other families – I've come across very few parents who have any real confidence in their ability to do a good job. They fall into the trap of measuring their performance against totally unrealistic 'ideals', and then feel inadequate when they don't match up. By far the most important lesson I've learnt about being a parent over the years is this: work hard and *trust yourself*.

This book isn't an *A to Z of Parenting*, with a complete index of exactly what to do and say in 1001 different situations. The *A to Z* kind of approach doesn't work, however much we'd like it to, because every parenting relationship is as different as the people in it. You and your family are unique. Your ages, the number of children you have, the position of each child in your family, your town, country, income, living conditions, friends, family and your relationship with your partner (if you have one) *all* make a big difference.

That's why I'm going to concentrate instead on the foundational principles of parenting. Without good foundations, it won't make any difference how fancy the house on top is: when it comes to the crunch, it'll still fall down. But if you've laid good foundations, what you choose to build on top will be secure. There are millions of different ways of being a good parent. The nuts and bolts of each unique approach often come down to individual style and flair, but they're all based on the same firm and solid principles, which are just like the scales every musician needs to know before they can improvise well and make up their own tune.

You *can* succeed as a parent. And the rest of this book is a series of nine more tips on how to do just that, and be the kind of parent your child is proud of. Feel free to ignore what's not relevant to you and apply what is.

But if you take only one thing away from reading this book, make it this: *there's no such thing as perfection, but you can be a* successful *parent. So work at it and trust yourself.*

Remember

- Becoming a parent totally transforms your life – you'll never be ready for it.
- The way a child is treated in their first few years can affect their whole life.
- Only people who aren't parents know for sure how to raise children properly.
- As a parent, you're on stage with no script and no prior rehearsals.
- However prepared you are, there's no getting away from daily improvisation.
- There's no such thing as a perfect parent, but you can be a great parent.
- The most important things you need to do are work hard and trust yourself.

Key principles

You can't be a perfect parent, but you can be a great one. So work at it and trust yourself.

How to achieve it

- Stop blaming yourself for past mistakes. You can't change yesterday, but tomorrow will be what you make it.
- Commit yourself to reading this book all the way through: it'll be time well spent.
- Decide what your aim as a parent is.
- Write yourself a short 'parent's job description'.

Tip Two

Be There

The house will be empty before you know it

> 'These are the good old days. Just wait and see.'
> Steve Turner, *Wait*

Life is 'Short and Sweet'

'I'd eat more ice cream and laugh more,' was the rather surprising reply of a senior and somewhat stern lawyer, with a reputation for working very long hours, when asked what she'd do differently if she had her years over again. 'I'd ride more rollercoasters,' she continued, 'sing louder in the bath, stay up late more often watching films with my friends, and spend a *lot* more time with my children!'

It's too easy to get trapped into living life on the basis that, though it's just one long hard slog today, one day it'll be easier and the slog will suddenly prove to have all been worth it. But the truth is, that day may never come.

Roy Castle, the popular entertainer, gave a press conference a short while before he died. The lung cancer that eventually claimed his life was already well advanced. A reporter from a national newspaper asked him, 'How does it feel to know that you only have a few months to live?' There was a stunned, awkward silence. Everyone wanted to know the answer, but no one else had dared ask the question. Then Roy smiled and said very softly, 'If I knew I had a few months to live, I'd be unique. You don't even know whether you'll still be alive this time tomorrow.'

Most of us assume that we'll be around for years to come. So we order our priorities accordingly. We put off doing *important* things because we're frankly too busy trying to do all the *urgent* things that keep piling up. We assume there'll be time to get round to the important things later on. So we work all hours in order to get a promotion at work, and tell ourselves that one day there'll be more time to watch our son play football, or that we'll find the time to collect conkers with him next year. There's so much housework to be done, and so many phone calls to make, that reading a bedtime story to our daughter or being there to help with her homework somehow gets pushed out.

But if we thought we only had a year to live, most of us would look at life differently. After all, nobody ever said on their deathbed, 'I wish I'd spent more time at the office.' So why do so many of us – men and women – act as though the office were more important than our family? And why do the rest of us so often allow the housework to tire us out, or get between us and our children?

> **'Nothing I've ever done has given me more joys and rewards than being a father to my children.'**
> Bill Cosby

Seize the day – don't let opportunities pass you by!

Children don't ask to be born. They're not around to be consulted. Deliberately or not, we invite our kids into our lives. Which, when you stop to think about it, means that once they're here, we *owe* it to them to give them the time, security, love and care they desperately need in order to thrive. From the moment they're born, we're effectively in debt to our children.

But more than that, the years you have with your children are all too short and irreplaceable. I once interviewed the famous American, Dr Billy Graham. Though suffering in the early stages of Parkinson's Disease, he was still very alert. Taking advantage of meeting one of the most famous men of the twentieth century, I asked what advice he could give me about how to make the most of my life. I was expecting something deep, something very deep – something so deep that it would take me months to get to grips with its full meaning. So I geared myself up and leaned in close to make sure I heard every word. There was a long silence that seemed to go on forever as he thought. Then finally he spoke: 'Life goes a lot quicker than you expect it to, so use each day wisely,' he said. That was it.

There aren't that many summer holidays, Bonfire nights, Easter bunny hunts, Pancake Days, conker collecting sessions and Christmas Eves left when your kids will still want to be with you. So the task of every wise parent is to grasp every opportunity they have during these fleeting early years firmly, and with both hands. Seize the day, because your children will soon be gone.

There'll come a day when they won't ask you to read stories to them any more, or want to sit on your lap and fall asleep, or play football with you, or get you to mend their bike. And strange as it may seem, all the things you struggle with now, you'll long for then. There will be days when you'll desperately want to read them a story . . . every word, all the way through! You'll wonder why you ever found reading *The Bumper Book of Bedtime Stories* (for the twenty-seventh time) so boring that you cheated and turned over three pages at once.

The years you have with your kids will be over and gone before you know it. Though it seems like only yesterday when I first held her in my arms, my eldest child has now left home for college, and my second child will soon be leaving home. I'd do well to remind myself of that fact every time he asks me to do something with him, or wants to talk, or just wants us to sit and watch TV together.

I may feel that I can't really afford the time right now to

I'VE FINALLY FOUND A FREE DAY TO GO TO THE CIRCUS – LIKE YOU WANTED...

BILL'S ROOM

THAT WAS TEN YEARS AGO, DAD – I'M TWENTY-ONE NOW.

meet all my children's demands. In light of all the other calls made on my time and energy, helping one of them with their homework or taking them to see a film may not seem to come very high on my list of priorities. But the boot will soon be on the other foot. One day, in the not too distant future, *I'll* be the one phoning to ask if they're too busy to pop home for the weekend. Rather than me finding time for them, they'll be trying (I hope!) to fit *me* into their hectic schedule and busy social diary.

'Time is money,' quipped Benjamin Franklin. But he was wrong. It isn't money. Time is far more valuable than money. The person with no money but lots of time has got everything to play for. But the person with no time and lots of money has nothing. Years ago, an agricultural advisor came across a peasant farmer taking a rest from his hard work under a tree. 'You should work harder, plant more,' he told him. 'Then you'd have more crops to sell, and you could hire other people to do the work for you.' 'What would I do then?' asked the farmer. 'Well, you could sit back and take things easy,' said the agricultural advisor. 'But that's what I'm doing now,' replied the farmer.

The house will be empty before you know it. Unlike money, time can't be stored or carried over to the next day or next year. And it won't stand still, no matter how busy you are at work or home or with other things – even if you're working towards a promotion in order to provide your family with more security, comfort and time in the future. So don't allow the housework, office, shopping, gym, pub, club, bingo hall, friends, church, car, or anything else to dominate your life so much that you don't have enough time left to spend with your kids. Don't put off making time for them now, hoping you'll be able to catch up later on. They'll be grown up and out of the home, and your opportunity will be gone forever. And you'll still be working all hours waiting for that 'big break'.

> **'Any fool can see the drawbacks of trying to combine parenthood with jobs without boundaries: the kind which suck you in, hype you up and render you unfit for any but colleagues' company.'**
>
> Libby Purves

Your job doesn't stop you finding the time: YOU do!

Of course, balancing your family with your work life and your other interests and responsibilities is never easy. There's no secret formula. It's a constant struggle. And just when you think you've got it sorted, something else comes along to throw everything back into confusion. It's a bit like walking a tight-rope. It's not a case of struggling initially to get your balance and then, having done so, finding that you're free to carry on regardless afterwards. Staying upright on the high wire is a *continuous* process of making tiny, but absolutely vital, adjustments.

It's easy to blame your job or the housework for your lack of time to spend with your children. It's also very easy, especially if you're a working mum, to get trapped into feeling really guilty about spending time at work and away from your kids. But the uncomfortable truth is that, contrary to popular opinion, the major tensions that arise because of competing home and work pressures aren't really to do with what kind of job or responsibilities you or your partner have. They're actually more to do with you and your *personality*.

It took me a long time to face up to this. Cornelia, on the other hand, having been married to me for over twenty years, has few illusions about me. She knows only too well that my workaholic tendencies and other irritating habits have little or nothing to do with what I do for a living. Instead, they're part of *me*. I'd have been every bit as difficult to live with if I'd become a bank manager, plumber, journalist, gardener, milkman or lawyer.

It's uncomfortable to admit it, but the truth is that when we blame 'work' for our failure to give our family the time and support they need, we're deluding ourselves. I'm not trying to dismiss work pressures. I know all too well how real they can be. It's just that going *out* to work doesn't excuse anyone from coming *home* to work.

It's not easy to find time for your family. But then, it's not easy finding the time to mix a passion for work with a passion for swimming, football, squash, bowling, fishing, golf or even the pub, club or gym. But busy working men and women have been managing it for years. High-flying career women and men don't have to be victims of their success. They can use their brains or money to find ways off the treadmill if they choose to. The very undramatic truth is that the decisions *can* be made . . . if only we're prepared to make them. As they say, 'Where there's a will, there's a way'.

Of course, if your job is no excuse for neglecting your family, neither is your personality. You can't hide from reality simply by calling yourself a 'workaholic'. That just doesn't let you off the hook. To be consistent, you'd need to be every bit as committed to your work as a parent as you are to your paid or domestic work. Don't give yourself a label you don't deserve.

Those of us who work outside the home can't just decide to turn off and block out the world when we get inside the front door. However much we might want to, we can't simply put our feet up in front of the TV and switch off. I can't excuse myself from communication, my share of the chores and involvement with my family on the grounds that I've been 'working hard all day'. It's a fatal mistake for someone in paid employment to behave as though 'work' stops the moment they leave the site or finish sifting through papers. The truth is that we need to work every bit as hard at our home life as we do in our workplace. What's more, making an effort at home isn't just the right thing to do – it's actually rewarding!

> **'Without a family, man, alone in the world, trembles with the cold.'**
>
> André Malraux

Don't believe your own publicity

In the film *Big*, Josh is a thirteen-year-old boy who makes a wish to become instantly big. The next morning, he wakes up to find that he has the body of a thirty-year-old. He's forced to leave home – after all, how do you tell your mother that, physically, you've aged twenty years in one night? Getting a job in a toy company, his child's-eye view of the world impresses his boss so much that he's promoted and given the task of testing and inventing new toys. Josh knows what children look for in a toy. After all, appearances aside, he's still only thirteen years old. But his priorities slowly change, and he becomes so involved in developing a new range of toys that he can't even find time to see his best friend, Billy. Eventually, Billy bursts into his office and interrupts a business call. 'That was important!' Josh shouts. 'Yeah?' Billy replies. 'Well, I'm your best friend. What's more important than that?'

Most of us like to think we're pretty important at work. So much so, in fact, that the danger is that we get mesmerised by our own sense of self-importance, and end up losing our grip on reality. Don't fool yourself: however crucial you think you are in your job, someone else always can, and eventually will, take your place. It's painful to admit it, but you're *not* indispensable. Except, that is, at home, where there's no replacement for you. You're the only mum or dad your kids have got. They actually *want* and *need* to be with you. They love you automatically, without any conditions. They want you to love them, and they're very forgiving of your past mistakes. They won't hold yesterday against you if today is fun.

Chris always saw his main task in the family as 'bringing home the bacon'. That's why, although he loved his kids, he allowed himself to spend so much time at the office. The problem was that, even when he *was* at home, more often than not he was preoccupied with urgent office paperwork. The way he saw it, he was working hard in order to give them a stable home and all the things he'd never had as a boy. One day, he figured, if he worked hard enough, he could retire early and enjoy all the 'returns' on this 'investment'. He'd be able to spend time with his wife and kids, knowing their future was secure.

So whenever they complained that they wished he was around more, he'd remind them, 'I'm doing this for you'. As far as he could see, his wife, Diane, had everything she could ever want. But for Diane, Chris – the man she'd married and wanted to spend her life with – was never there to enjoy them with her, or to talk to about the things that really mattered to her. She loved him, but felt abandoned.

At first she resented all the time he spent working, but Diane slowly learnt that she had to detach herself from Chris emotionally if she was to survive. She threw herself wholeheartedly into the role of being a full-time mother, and gradually built up her own circle of friends. Being busy helped cover over her loneliness. And then, as the kids grew and became more independent, she pushed herself to get involved with voluntary work for a local charity. She was good at what she did, very popular and much in demand.

Eventually, at fifty, Chris took his early retirement. He had a comfortable pension and looked forward to enjoying life with his family . . . only to discover they weren't there. His children had all left home and made lives for themselves elsewhere. And even when they came to visit, he found it almost as hard to talk to them as they did to him. There seemed to be so little common ground between them – they just ran out of things to say. And Diane, who had once had all the time in the world for him, was now always out, always busy, always preoccupied, and so remote. This wasn't the woman he'd married. She was a total stranger. Chris felt alone. Was this really what he'd worked so hard and so long for?

In the film *Beethoven*, George and his wife Alice argue about the family dog, which is ruining his business plans. 'My dreams are going down the drain and you're worried about a dog?' he yells. 'Your family is going down the drain and you're worried about a dream!' she replies.

The truth is that, like it or not, how you're doing at work just *isn't* a big priority for your kids. If they're under thirteen, they already think you're the greatest parent on the planet. If anything were to happen to you, they're convinced that the world would immediately stop turning. And if they're over thirteen, they're unimpressed by what you do at work anyway. What you do *for them* is far more important. They understand that you have to work, but what they're really interested in is your time. They don't care about your public profile, your promotion or the size of your pay packet. But they *do* care about you, so make time for them today while you still can.

'Don't get into the habit of working long hours. When it's a habit, it ceases to be a virtue.'

Aphorism quoted in *The Sunday Telegraph*

Quality time includes quantity time

In the 1980s, power-dressed Yuppies gave birth to phrases like 'Okay, Yah', 'Let's do lunch', 'I've got a small window in my diary' and 'Let's spend some quality time together'. It became fashionable to believe that it wasn't so much the *quantity* of time you spent with your children that mattered, but rather the *quality* of that time. High-flying city executives convinced themselves that if they 'diaried in' some 'power time' with their kids – which they filled with intense, quality activity – then they'd have adequately fulfilled their obligations as mums or dads. But sadly, 'quality time' was often nothing more than an empty excuse for giving children far less time than they really needed.

One of the clearest ways children have of measuring the *quality* of time you spend with them is by looking at its sheer *quantity*. Actually, that makes a lot of sense. After all, when you love someone, you want to spend as much time with them as you can. So if your children get the impression that you don't want to spend time with them, it's logical for them to assume that you don't really love them, whatever else you might say to them or buy for them. Your kids want your *presence*, not your *presents*. (However, it's also important to remember that it doesn't make any difference *how* much time you spend with your kids if, in doing so, you give them the impression that you don't really want them around, or that you're bored by their company. Your child can feel neglected even if you're there the whole time.)

When someone casually asks in a passing conversation, 'How are you?', what's your reply? 'OK, thanks.' It's the standard answer, even if the truth is actually very different. Very few of us wear our hearts on our sleeves. For most of us, it takes a huge amount of courage, and lots of time, to feel safe enough to open up and tell someone our innermost thoughts, feelings and problems. Trust isn't usually built quickly. The deep issues

WHAT'S YOUR MOST ABIDING FAMILY MEMORY?

THE WHOLE FAMILY SITTING ROUND WONDERING WHEN WE'D FIND TIME TO MAKE FAMILY MEMORIES.

and important questions – the things that matter most to children – trickle out because a parent is *there*. In fact, kids have a habit of asking the deepest questions at the oddest and most inappropriate moments.

Important conversations don't often happen on cue or in 'diaried time'. Sitting your child down face to face for a 'quality time' chat about their problems is very intimidating, and will rarely produce the required result. But every now and then, in a less threatening, 'neutral' environment – when you're making the tea, or fixing shelves, or out swimming, or even watching TV – you'll find that they raise all sorts of unexpected and important subjects 'out of the blue'. After an hour spent helping you try to put together a piece of IKEA furniture that's designed to be assembled in less than five minutes, your son or daughter will suddenly start telling you about what upset them at school last week, or about what they want to do with their life, or about the older boys or girls who talked about taking drugs at the end of term disco. For the mum or dad who invests *quantity* time, suddenly there's an opportunity for a *quality* conversation.

Most of the best conversations I've had with my kids about things like careers, racism, bullying, love, failure, success, honesty, relationships, money, justice – and many more – have started just like this. Just being around your children sends them the message, 'I'm comfortable with you. I enjoy your company. I'm glad you're here.' And they're reassured that it's safe for them to ask intimate questions or talk about personal things without fear of being rejected.

The truth is that, in almost every area of life, *quality* only comes when *quantity* time has been invested. Take gardening, for instance. Creating a beautiful garden takes a lot of time and effort. There are beds to be dug, seeds to be sown, weeds to be pulled, grass to be mown, plants to be watered, trees to be pruned, and hedges to be clipped. Of course, you can pay someone to do it for you, but there's no short cut to horticultural perfection. Someone has to put in some very hard work. No time in, no quality out! And though *you* might turn a blind eye to the 'jungle' outside your front or back door, a neglected garden is obvious to everyone else.

Parenting is even more time-consuming than gardening. And unlike your garden, children are very fussy about who takes care of them. For working parents, and especially single parents, daycare and childminding facilities are often essential. But although these can provide overstretched parents with a few hours in which to work or relax, they can never replace the time they need to spend with their children. So it's no good fetching your child from nursery school and assuming they've received their 'recommended daily dose' of human contact. Rather than reducing a parent's need to spend time with their kids, leaving them in the capable hands of babysitters and childcare professionals actually makes finding this time even more important.

> **'If I had to say what I thought was one of the most important things about being a dad, it's "being around".'**
>
> Michael Rosen, *Goodies & Daddies*

To find the time, start small and slowly build up

Our children *need* our time. And if it really mattered enough to us, we'd find it for them. That rather uncomfortable truth is the same, however legitimate our excuses sound. The problem is that, very often, we fail to grasp just how important our attention is to them. And of course, one of the main reasons for this mistake is that we don't spend enough time with them for it to become obvious to us.

It's a Catch 22 situation. Giving our kids time comes low on our agenda because we don't spend long enough with them to realise how much they need. And because it's low on our agenda, we never have the time to discover that we need to change our priorities. Until, that is, it's too late.

Of course, knowing all this is one thing, but actually making the time is another. It's like sport. We all want to be fit, strong and healthy. But for the vast majority of us, being out of shape is a habit we'll never change, for one simple reason: we don't get up at 6 o'clock every morning and put in the effort to do the training.

A commentator on the 1996 Olympic Games in Atlanta described them as an event where 'the world's fittest performed for the world's fattest'. And as most Britons worried about catching 'Mad Cow Disease' from eating BSE-infected beef, one doctor warned that the public was far more at risk from the onset of 'Mad Couch Disease'. You were more likely to get ill from watching too much sport on TV, he argued, than from eating beef. Spectating is now by far the most popular and dangerous sport there is. We're becoming a nation who are so keen on sport that we spend endless hours sitting in front of the TV, watching *other* people taking exercise rather than taking it ourselves. It's true what they say about football: 22,000 people in need of exercise watch 22 people in need of a rest!

But in exactly the same way, and for the same reasons, many of us end up settling for being spectators in our kids' lives. Making time for your family requires the same kind of dedicated, disciplined effort and activity as training for sport. The problem is that so many good intentions fall flat because the goals we set are just too ambitious. Just as you shouldn't start trying to get fit by pledging to run a half-marathon every morning, so it's equally daft to promise to make radical changes to your lifestyle overnight. Even if you manage an initial burst of enthusiasm, this kind of drastic change rarely works in the long run. It's much better to build up your 'family fitness' slowly, in a well disciplined but not overly demanding way.

Don't promise to make unrealistic changes to your diary or working habits that are just too much, too soon. Instead, set some attainable goals. Learn to walk before you try to run. As all successful business people know, goals must be realistic and sensible. Rather than trying to get home from work two hours earlier every day, have a go at thirty minutes, even if it's only twice a week, so you can read your child a story before they go to bed. Rather than pledging to spend every night in and take every weekend off to be with your children, dedicate one night a week and one weekend a month as uninterruptible family time when you do something together. The secret is to start small, but make it a priority, and apply the same dedication to achieving your objective at home as you would to an objective at work.

Don't be fooled into seeing the task ahead as so daunting that you just put it off. Tomorrow never comes, so begin today. The clock is ticking and time is running out. So whatever you do and however you do it, start making time for your kids today. I've slowly learnt that it's easier to set time aside and not allow other things to get in the way if we plan in advance to do something as a family: treats, outings, holidays or surprises. I've also learnt that what we do isn't half as important as the fact that we do it together.

But it's also important to spend time with each child individually. I often take one of our children to breakfast on

WHOOPS! LOOKS LIKE DAD'S PLANNED ANOTHER SURPRISE OUTING...

TRAP DOOR

Saturdays. We usually go to the local McDonald's, because it's cheap and cheerful, but it's still special. It's a great time to talk by ourselves, laugh, tell jokes and catch up on things without all the distractions of home. And occasionally I take one of our daughters out on a 'date' to a restaurant somewhere – just her and me. Or book to go to a football match with one of the boys. None of it needs to cost the earth. You don't have to take your kids to the Ritz to make it special. You just have to take the time. As they say, the way kids spell 'love' is T.I.M.E. And the funny thing is, however reluctant you are to do it at first, you'll probably end up enjoying it even more than they do.

> **'My dad was always there for me and my brother, and I want my kids to have the same kind of dad – a dad they will remember. Being a dad is the most important thing in my life.'**
>
> Kevin Costner

A family is a lot more than just flatmates

Question: What's the difference between a family and a group of flatmates?
Answer: Commitment to each other, and time spent demonstrating it.

In the film *Gregory's Girl*, Gregory is a seventeen-year-old growing up on a Glasgow housing estate. The only things that really matter to him are football and girls. But one day, he almost succeeds in getting himself run over by his father on the way to school. The chance encounter turns into an opportunity to catch up on family news. 'Your mother,' his father says. 'You remember your mother? She asked me how you were. I said we'd passed each other in the hallway last Thursday.' Eventually, Gregory and his dad make a date for breakfast one morning the following week.

Gregory and his parents live in the *same* house. In the film, this situation is funny – after all, it's a comedy. But on a less dramatic scale, the same situation happens every day in millions of real-life families . . . only then it's a tragedy.

When you spend time with your kids, you help create good family memories for them – memories that play a huge part in establishing their security and stability, or lack of it, in later years. The truth is that memories which remind people that they have always been loved help create a powerful emotional base on which to build the rest of their lives. So wherever they go and whatever they do, these memories will go a long way to providing them with an unshakeable feeling of inner security.

One summer, Cornelia and I arranged a treasure hunt for our children while we were on holiday. We bought some rather inexpensive 'treasure' we knew they'd like. We got Joshua a fountain pen for school, Daniel a key ring, Emily a silver ring and Abigail a necklace. We wrote out a series of clues and hid them in the house and fields around where we were staying. Solving Clue One led them to Clue Two, and so on. When the end of the trail was finally reached, they were all extremely happy with the spoils of their hard work. (And Cornelia and I got the time it took them, a good two hours, to ourselves in peace!) But the best thing is that, long after the 'treasure' has been lost or broken, the memory of a happy childhood day will live on. In fact, I wouldn't be surprised if in another thirty years' time or so, a new generation of junior Chalkes is sent on a similar hunt, and even, on their return, told the story of the 'Summer of '96'.

And each year, after we get our holiday photos back, we all sit around the kitchen table cutting them up to make a collage. We design it in one of those huge clip frames, and when it's finished, we hang it up somewhere in the house. It's fun making the collage together. And more than that, when one of us stops to look at it on the wall every now and then, it brings back lots of great memories once more.

But don't pay too much attention to what the Chalkes do or don't do. (You ought to know, anyway, that not everything we do quite works out as we planned it. We have our fair share of disasters, just like everyone else!) The point is that what *you* choose to do with *your* family is actually far less important than the fact that you all do it together. In fact, it doesn't matter whether it's camping in the back garden, going swimming, playing snooker, having a weekend away, eating out, driving to the seaside, playing tennis, watching football, playing Monopoly or any one of 1001 other activities. The important thing is, by taking the time to do *something* together as a family, and to enjoy each other's company, you're cementing relationships, building good memories, and proving to your children that your love is more than just words.

Remember

- Life is short, so don't waste it.
- The years you have with your children are irreplaceable, and gone too soon.
- Work as hard at being a parent as you do at anything else that matters to you.
- The only place you're really indispensable is at home.
- Quality time is the product of quantity time.
- Develop the habit of planning time for your children.
- Start building good family memories together now.

Key principles

Make time for your children NOW!

How to achieve it

- Book an evening each week to 'waste' time with your kids.
- Take your child out to breakfast this weekend.
- Plan a surprise outing for your family. (If you have a partner, tell them first!)
- Plan to have at least one mealtime together each week with the TV off and the phone unplugged.

Tip Three

Be Unambiguous

Don't place conditions on your love

'A woman who is loved always has success.'

Vicki Baum

What is happiness?

Every parent wants to give their child the very best start in life they can. If that weren't important to you, you wouldn't be reading this book. The fact that you are, and that you've got this far, shows you care. But the sixty-four-thousand-dollar question, of course, is: What *is* the best for your child, and how do you go about giving it to them?

What are your ambitions for your child? We all want our kids to be happy, but what *is* happiness? Is it an expensive, high-quality education guaranteed to catapult them to the top of their chosen profession? Is it having every toy they could ever want? Is it having a wardrobe full of the latest clothes to make them popular with friends, or the freedom to do what they want? Or is it something else altogether?

Your definition of what it means to be happy will shape and colour your child's entire life, so it's vital to get it right. But what *is* happiness, and how *can* we create it for our children, ensuring that they're happy?

Many parents see happiness as 'success'. They want their children to get to the top in life, and stay there. But there's a problem with this. Throughout their lives your children, just like you, will unfortunately find themselves being accepted or rejected on the basis of how they perform. Most people they meet will have time for them, or not, because of what they can offer or deliver. It's a familiar story. From the schoolkids who'll 'be your best friend forever' as long as you give them sweets or stickers, to celebrities surrounded by 'hangers on'. It's the way the world works, and it's a very hard lesson to learn. But the truth stares us all in the face: many people only want us in life when we're 'successful'. So like it or not, your children will slowly discover that most people are interested in them because of their looks, their skills, their contacts or their money – in short, because they have something they want.

It's a parent's job to be an exception to this rule. Your task is to love and accept your child not for what they can achieve but for who they are, with no strings attached, and to make sure they receive this message. Parents must be able to say to their children, 'I love you because I love you, and that's all there is to it!'

It's this kind of unconditional, or 'no strings attached', love that we all need to be happy. If we never receive it, we end up heading through life constantly struggling to please people in order to make them love us, and crippled by our fear that we'll accidentally do something to make them stop loving us and reject us. In fact, you can have money, fame, power, status and success, but if you don't feel loved and accepted unconditionally, you won't be satisfied, and will never be truly happy.

How many rock, film or sports stars can you think of who've had money, fame, power, status and success and yet *still* not been happy? The problem is that, if we've never known unconditional love, we can so easily get our three basic needs as human beings – love, security and significance – confused with sex, money and power. And the result is always disastrous.

At the extreme end, not being sure that you're loved with no strings attached can lead to tragic illnesses like anorexia and bulimia. And in 1994, the Joseph Rowntree Foundation reported that children who felt rejected by their parents were more likely to be sexually promiscuous as teenagers than those whose homes were secure. In other words, if your kids aren't sure you love them unconditionally, they'll most likely go looking for love elsewhere. And very often, they'll end up looking in all the wrong places and settle for a highly conditional love – to their cost.

> **'Everybody knows that a good mother gives her children a feeling of trust and stability ... Somehow even her clothes feel different to her children's hands from anybody else's clothes. Only to touch her skirt or her sleeve makes a troubled child feel better.'**
>
> Katherine Butler Hathaway

Unconditional love comes automatically at first

Loving their children unconditionally isn't hard for most parents. In fact, it comes naturally. Even dads who don't feel a tinge of excitement about becoming a parent in the months leading up to the birth of their child melt when they first catch sight of their new-born baby. I don't think I really appreciated how I would feel about being a dad until I held my first child in my arms. But from the moment I did, I knew that I loved her. And I knew that I'd *always* love her, no matter what she did or failed to do in her life. I didn't love her because of what she could offer me or do for me, or because of her personality. I loved her because I loved her, and for no other reason. That's unconditional love.

There's an instant, natural, biological bond of love between mums and their kids. And even for dads, who haven't carried the child for nine months, there's a kind of irresistible magnetism. A baby's big eyes, little face, gawky behaviour and vulnerability all draw out our parental instincts. In fact, some scientists say that babies deliberately evolved to look like this in order to trigger our parental and loving instincts, and to get us oohing and ahhing.

And the feeling isn't one-sided. Children grow up instinctively loving and trusting their parents. They want and need our attention and acceptance. But though toddlers still take it for granted that you love them, they'll naturally begin to question all of their previous assumptions as they grow older . . . including your love for them. And tragically, if we're not careful, without ever meaning to, we end up sending them all the wrong signals.

It's *because* we want the best for our kids that we push them to do all kinds of things that they don't always want to do. From eating their greens to practising the piano, and from going to bed on time to going to school when there's a maths test – that's part of why a parent is there. Children rarely understand the long-term consequences of their actions, and don't usually have enough facts and experience to take major decisions for themselves. We can all think of a time as we were growing up when our parent or parents made us do something we didn't understand and resented, but which we later came to see was wise and are now grateful for.

But though it's every parent's responsibility to play this role, the way in which we choose to handle our part is vital. We can get it so right or so wrong! The problem is that, if we're not careful, all we end up communicating to our kids is criticism. Because we want them to do well, we're keen to point out their mistakes and explain how they could do better. At the same time, we assume they *know* we love them. After all, if we didn't, why would we take so much interest in them and their performance? And the older our kids get, the more severe our 'guidance' tends to become, and the less we actually communicate to them how much we love them. 'They know I love them,' we explain. But the question is: how do they know?

> **'We don't love qualities, we love a person.'**
>
> Jacques Maritain

The Man in the White Suit

My friend Tony's job takes him around the world. He once found himself sitting on a plane across the aisle from a ten-year-old girl, returning to her family after a term away at boarding school. At first he was surprised that she was flying alone in Business Class. But he slowly became fascinated by the fact that she was eating and drinking absolutely everything that was put in front of her, and then summoning the flight attendants for even more. Ignoring the work he was meant to be doing, he watched her closely from behind his newspaper.

She was obviously making the most of her first flight on her own. But even so, as a seasoned flyer, Tony knew that it was very unwise to eat quite so much. Sooner or later, what goes down in such large quantities has to come back up again! Sure enough, by the time the plane touched down she was looking decidedly green. And as she walked down the gangway, she threw up all over her dress.

Following her down the steps, Tony could see a man in an immaculately pressed and expensive white suit waiting on the tarmac, waving at her. From the look on his face, and the excitement in his eyes at seeing her, Tony could tell he was her father. But what surprised him was how, even though he could see the state of her dress, he raced toward her, bent down and threw his arms around his daughter without a moment's hesitation, enfolding her in a massive hug. As they walked back to the terminal together, his suit now permanently stained with vomit, all Tony could see in the man's eyes was joy at being with his daughter again. That's unconditional love.

Even if we regularly tell our kids we love them for who they are, it's no good if everything else we say and do sends them a different message. We want our kids to do well, and we know that this means giving them a push to succeed. But tragically, the way in which so many parents do this is almost guaranteed to backfire. If our kids believe, or even suspect, that we love them more when they succeed than when they fail, they'll naturally try to succeed in order to win our approval. But in the process, they'll stop believing that we love them unconditionally and start to link love with achievement. When that happens, in pushing our children to succeed, we'll end up failing them as parents.

One of the biggest problems with expecting your child to succeed or come first all the time is, of course, that no one actually does. Even really gifted children will fail sooner or later. So if your child's self-esteem is pinned to success, and measured in those terms, they're doomed to live their whole life with a sense of failure and guilt. As a result, they're likely to feel unloved and unworthy – condemned to a life of anxiety, jealousy, bitterness, doubt, insecurity and bad losing.

The Bible says, 'Be happy with those who're happy, and sad with those who're sad.' But how many people spend their lives with it all the other way round: only happy when they hear someone else has failed, and threatened by anyone else's success simply because of their sense of insecurity and jealousy?

It's perfectly natural to have high hopes, expectations and standards for your kids. But a problem arises if they begin to link these with your love for them. Then, no matter how well-intentioned they may be, these hopes, expectations and standards become crippling. And the ironic thing is that, whatever level of success your kids reach in childhood or later life, it'll never be enough to satisfy them. They'll always think you expect more, so they'll never be able to relax and enjoy the ride. Rather than being in control of their lives and able to enjoy the fruits of their success, they'll be constantly driven by the need to try to live up to 'your' expectations. If your son feels that your love for him is linked to his performance as a footballer, for example, making his school team won't convince him of your love. In the end, even scoring the winning goal as England captain in a World Cup final will be a hollow victory. He'll still feel he blew it by not scoring a hat-trick or becoming European Footballer of the Year.

Peter, a friend of mine, is at the very top of his profession: wealthy, successful, charming and generous. But he's deeply

unhappy. For more than twenty years he's been driven by the need to impress his dad, convinced that he still doesn't measure up to his expectations. Unfortunately, his dad is dead. I'm sure that if he were still alive, he'd be the proudest man on earth. But by giving Peter the impression, as a boy, that his love was conditional on achievement and success, he's condemned him to a life of empty ambition.

> **'There is no cure for birth or death save to enjoy the interval.'**
>
> George Santayana

Unconditional love gives your children strength to live their lives

If life is a journey, love that's *conditional* on achievement is all about arriving at your final destination. You receive acceptance if and when you cross the finishing line. But the problem is, the only real 'finishing line' in life is death. Even if you reach 'the top', there's always another peak to strive for above the one you're on. And there's always the danger of toppling off. But *unconditional* love – loving your child for who they are, not what they do – is about giving them the strength and inner resources to enjoy the journey, rather than simply the satisfaction of reaching their destination. By showing your kids that you love them unconditionally, you're proving to them that they're intrinsically valuable and individually unique human beings, quite apart from their performance.

In one episode of *Star Trek: The Next Generation*, a Federation scientist named Maddox plans to disassemble Commander Data. Data is an android: a machine built to walk, talk and think just like a human being. But since his creator is now dead, Maddox wants to take Data to bits in order to understand how he works, and then make more androids like him. However, although he promises to put him back together again afterwards,

Data isn't convinced. So he refuses to be disassembled because, he argues, there is nothing like him in the universe, and if Maddox failed to reassemble him properly, then something unique would be lost.

This is the same message we want our children to understand. Without them being arrogant, we want them to know that the world is a better place for having them in it, and that we love them for who they are, not what they can do for us. If a parent offers their child love on any other basis, however well-meaning, it'll be shortsighted and ultimately destructive.

In the film *Dead Poets Society*, Neil Perry's dad constantly pushes him to get good grades and become a doctor: a good, stable, prestigious job. But when Neil lands a lead role in a local production of *A Midsummer Night's Dream*, he suddenly knows what he wants to do with his life: become an actor. When his father finds out, he's furious. He wants the best for his son, and is convinced that this entails him becoming a doctor, so he decides to send him to a stricter and more regimented school that will knock this silly passion for acting out of him and focus his mind on more constructive study. But to Neil, it seems that his dad will only love him if he fulfils his dad's dreams and ambitions. Why can't he accept him just for who he is? When he finally realises his dad will never allow him to be an actor, he becomes increasingly depressed. His life is pointless, and he can't see a way out. In the end, tragically, he takes his own life with his father's gun.

Neil's problem is simple: if his dad can't love him as an actor, it means he can't love *him* at all. And he desperately needs his dad's love and acceptance. In fact, the truth is that his dad loves him a lot. It's just that his expectations are so high that his love appears totally conditional.

So how can a parent motivate their kid to unleash their potential and at the same time make sure they know that they're loved unconditionally?

'Cry for the millions who live their whole lives driven by the desire for approval they never received from their mum and dad.'

Anonymous

The confidence to lose

Life is competitive. Like it or not, that's the way it is. From school classes to job interviews, we're all surrounded by competition all of the time. There's nothing we can do to change that. But because no parent wants their child to come last, they tend to react in one of two ways. They either try to shield their kids from any form of competition, which of course just postpones the inevitable, or they deliberately groom them for success. Both approaches are shortsighted. The problem is that failure, like competition, is inevitable. Whoever you are, you can't win everything. Your children are going to spend their whole lives meeting people who're faster, cleverer, richer, kinder, more attractive and more inventive than they are. It doesn't matter how good a tennis player, footballer, artist, musician, writer, speaker, racing driver or accountant they are, there'll always be someone faster, better or younger waiting to take their place.

A constant theme of Hollywood Westerns was the gunfighter – the 'fastest draw in town' – who had to keep defending his

title . . . and with it his life! Young men, convinced they were faster and better than he was, forced him into gunfights in the streets, getting themselves killed in the process. For the gunfighter, staying at the top of his profession was just as hard as getting there in the first place, and sooner or later he was bound to lose his edge: permanently. Don't set your child up with the same kind of problem!

In the same way, the first thing to learn about getting on a horse is how to fall off safely, because however good you are, you *will* fall off. So if you teach your kids how to succeed, but not how to cope with failure or just plain ordinariness, you're not actually doing them any long-term favours.

I have a friend whose son is a good runner. In fact, he's a very good runner. And when he was chosen to compete for his school in a regional final, his parents couldn't have been more proud. Although he's not big for his age, he's fast. To get selected, he had to beat older and stronger boys. He trained hard, and was in peak mental and physical condition. He could see himself crossing the finishing line, and he did . . . last. His opponents were the best in the region, and all of them were older, taller and quicker than he was. He was devastated. When he got home afterwards, he ran straight up to his room and shut himself in, convinced that he'd let himself and everyone else down. When his dad tried to talk to him later, he looked more unhappy than ever. As they sat on his bed, he looked hard at the floor.

'Did you give it your best shot?' his dad asked.

'Yes,' he replied. He couldn't even blame the result on him having an 'off day'.

'Then I'm proud of you,' his dad told him, getting up to leave. 'All I care about is that you give everything your best effort. It's great to win, but there's no shame at all in losing if you've put everything you can into it.'

As his dad reached the door, the son said, 'You really love me, don't you?'

And he does. We're always proud of our children when they do well, but doing well doesn't always mean coming first. It means applying yourself to the task, and using your abilities to their full potential: giving it your best shot. And as parents, we need to make sure that even when our kids don't win or succeed, they still know that we love them just as much anyway.

> **'Love is a passion entirely unrelated to our merits.'**
>
> Paul Eldridge, *House of Glass*

Unconditional love is the gift you can afford ... whoever you are

Eric Liddell, hero of the film, *Chariots of Fire*, surprised everyone at the 1924 Olympic Games by winning the 400 yards against stiff competition. But it was knowing he'd achieved a personal best that gave him the most pleasure, not the Gold medal. He'd previously refused to enter the 100 yards heats, his chosen distance, because they fell on a Sunday, so he'd been automatically disqualified from running in the final. As a result, he moved overnight from being a national hero to being Public Enemy Number One. The British athletic authorities put huge pressure on him to run in the Sunday race. If he'd been motivated primarily by a desire to please others, he'd almost certainly have won the 100 yards race, but in doing so he'd have lost his integrity.

Your children need to know that being good at something is its own reward. At the end of the day, the reason for doing well isn't actually to make others proud of you, but to realise your own potential. That means that the *real* competition isn't with other people, but with yourself, which is why the motto of the Olympic Games emphasises that 'it's not the winning that counts, but the taking part'.

As parents, we want the best for our children. We want to

give them the ability to cope with life's inevitable ups and downs. But to achieve this, we have to help them to do more than just discover and build on their strengths. As strange as it seems, if that's all they can do, they'll be extremely vulnerable. We also need to help them to accept and live with their weaknesses and limitations, and be at peace with themselves.

Since before they could speak, I developed the habit of asking my kids how much I loved them. Eventually, they knew the answer off by heart: 'up to the sky and forever'. As each of them has got older and wiser, they've sat me down quietly to explain, 'Well, you see, Dad, the thing is . . . the sky is really high. In fact, it never actually ends . . .' And slowly, they've got the point. No matter what they do, or don't do, or what they become, I'll always love them more than they know.

Children play better, learn better, concentrate better, relate better, laugh more, give more and love more when they feel unconditionally loved than when they don't. This doesn't mean that they'll be straight-A students or Olympic-standard athletes. It's just that if they know you love them whatever, they're bound to be happy and content with themselves. If your child knows that they're loved in this way, it will act as a kind of internal compass to help steer them through all life's inevitable knocks and disappointments.

Unconditional love is the greatest gift any parent can ever give their children. And the funny thing is that it's the one gift that every parent can always afford to give their child. It doesn't matter how rich or poor you are – we're all on a level playing field. By clearly and persistently showing and proving to your children that you'll always love them, no matter what they do, you can grant them the self-confidence, security and self-esteem they'll need to be happy throughout life's journey.

Remember

- To be happy, your children need to know that you love them unconditionally.
- Words aren't enough: what you do says much more.
- Your kids need constant reassurance that you love them for who they are, not what they do.
- Never link your love for your children with your expectations of them.
- Showing your kids that you love them no matter what lets them know they're valuable and builds up their self-esteem.
- Proving to your kids that you love them helps them cope with inevitable failure and disappointment, and gives them the confidence to try again.

Key principles

Love your children for who they are, not what they do, and make sure they understand this.

How to achieve it

- Make sure you tell your kids TODAY how much you love them, and how valuable they are to you.
- Now tell them again! Remember, it takes a long time for the message to sink in.
- Reassure your kids you love them when they've done badly, even if this just means sitting with them.
- Make sure you don't ever give the impression that you love them because they succeed.

Be Firm

The positive role that discipline plays

'Raising kids is part joy and part guerrilla warfare.'

Ed Asner

Discipline is an essential tool for parenting

One South African Game Reserve has a big problem. Experts there are worried about some of their young male elephants, who are behaving very badly. They're attacking tourists and trying to mate with female white rhinos. In fact, over a period of three years, nineteen rhinos have been gored to death, and one rogue elephant even killed the professional hunter who was sent in to shoot it. Experts are unanimous: the young elephants' unusually aggressive and violent behaviour is the result of their never having been disciplined and nurtured by a 'matriarchal female'. Put simply, they're missing their mothers!

The problem was that the young elephants were moved from one Game Reserve to another without their mothers or any other family members. Since they'd already been weaned, the park authorities assumed it was safe to move them. But they were wrong . . . and the results have been disastrous. Eddie Koch, who's looked into the problem, summed it all up: 'Like children, young elephants need discipline if they are to grow up as responsible members of society.' The young elephants 'turned delinquent because they have never been taken in hand by their elders'.

Discipline has a bad press. For most of us, it's a word that conjures up Victorian images of children being 'seen but not heard'. A century ago, parents were stern, table manners were impeccable and punishment was severe. 'Spare the rod, spoil the child' was the household motto. Discipline was all about punishment, and punishment was all about the cane, the belt or – if your parents were the soft type – just the slipper!

The problem with this is that the Victorians have left many of us still believing that 'discipline = punishment': nothing more and nothing less. Just yesterday I was reading a book on parenting, published only last year, in which three whole chapters were given over to discipline. Unfortunately, *all* of them were about how to punish children for their mistakes . . . usually with a wooden spoon on the backside!

But seeing punishment and discipline as the same thing creates another very destructive problem: love and discipline are then seen as contradictory. You can do one or the other, but you can't love your child and discipline them in the same breath. As a result of this misunderstanding, some parents choose to underplay the role of discipline, while others steer well clear of it altogether because they see it as cruel, negative and unloving. And then, often too late, they end up wondering why they can't do anything to control their children's behaviour.

The truth is that discipline and punishment aren't the same thing at all. Discipline is about a whole lot more than just punishment. In fact, punishment is only a very small part of healthy discipline, which should be an overwhelmingly *positive* experience. And love, far from being something that contradicts discipline, is its motivation, its cause and its goal.

Discipline should be the framework and encouragement that a loving parent creates for their child in order to help them gradually learn how to control their behaviour, and develop self-discipline. Discipline should be an enabler: a creative force designed to build maturity and consistency, helping children fit into society without being swamped by it. Discipline should give your children the self-control they need to manage what they do, both now and in the future.

> **'I have found that if you love until it hurts, there is no more hurt, only love.'**
>
> Mother Teresa

Discipline doesn't stifle freedom, it creates it

It's a mistake to think of discipline as the enemy of freedom – it's actually its friend. The young South African elephants weren't given extra freedom by their undisciplined upbringing. Instead, its result was stress, insecurity and a lack of self-discipline in their lives. If their mothers and older male elephants had been there to keep them in line, teaching them the boundaries of acceptable elephant behaviour, then these 'juvenile delinquents' would not only have helped create a normal family life, they'd have enjoyed it as well.

When I was ten years old, I learnt to play the piano. I wasn't very good. Actually, to tell the truth, I was awful. The reason was, I hated the lessons. I did just about everything I could to avoid having to sit down and practise the dreaded scales and boring set pieces. I wanted to be able to play the piano, but I didn't like the discipline of practice. (I drove my teacher up the wall . . . and, in the end, literally to tears!)

If you listen to me playing the piano today, the results of all this are obvious. My style is lumpy, to put it mildly. Instead of dancing across the keyboard like butterflies, my fingers stumble and plod laboriously. Discipline in learning to play the piano wouldn't have *restricted* my freedom – it would actually have *created* it. If I'd practised properly, I'd now be able to sit down in front of our piano at home and play to my heart's content. Discipline as a child would have brought me freedom as an adult. But as it is, since they can't bear the awful racket I make whenever I try to play our piano, my family has banned me from going anywhere near it!

When I was ten, I thought discipline was the opposite of freedom. I thought that whenever my parents stopped me from doing anything I wanted to do, or made me do something I didn't want to do, all they were doing was taking away my freedom. Now, of course, I can see that I was wrong. With the benefit of hindsight, I know that the discipline my parents instilled in me when I was younger has given me the freedom I enjoy now. The truth is that real freedom is never the *enemy* of discipline – it's the *product* of it.

The problem is that, as someone once complained, life has to be lived forwards, but can only be understood backwards. This, of course, is why no child (however bright) ever fully understands the real value of good discipline until they're older . . . so you shouldn't expect yours to!

If the big question is, 'Why should I discipline my children?', the answer is that the aim of all discipline should be to build your child's self-discipline, and therefore their self-esteem. Good discipline will help them develop as confident people who're in control of their actions and emotions, and ultimately their lives. It will help them to become the architects of their future instead of its victims. But tragically, when parents are either undisciplined or consistently unfair in the way they discipline their children, things fall a long way short of this.

> **'My father was frightened of his mother, I was frightened of my father, and I'm damned well going to make sure that my children are frightened of me.'**
>
> King George V

'Undisciplined discipline' is a recipe for disaster

If we're not careful, what we call 'discipline' can degenerate into nothing more than a chance for us to work off our anger or frustration with our children for their mistakes and failings. And even worse than that, sometimes the 'discipline' that a parent hands out has little or nothing to do with their *child's* behaviour at all. Instead, lack of sleep, exhaustion and pressure at home or work has got the better of them and they're looking for a soft target to take it all out on. Their kids fit the bill perfectly.

At the end of a long day, it's easy for a parent to view their child's actions as 'the last straw'. Whether it's making a noise or making a mess, asking questions or wanting help, it all just seems like too much to cope with. So they end up lashing out, either verbally or physically. Their kids find themselves on the receiving end of their frustration, being shouted at, bawled at, grounded, banished, threatened, shaken, slapped, beaten, or even kicked or punched, for tiny violations of the family code – or worse still, for no reason at all except the unpredictable mood swings of their parent. It's not their fault: they're just the unfortunate 'victim' who happens to be in the wrong place at the wrong time.

Often, of course, when a parent calms down, they realise what they've done and are filled with guilt and remorse. They

PARENTS NEED A DISCIPLINED APPROACH TO HANDLING DISCIPLINE.

vow never to do the same thing again. But there's a danger that this kind of behaviour can develop into a habit. It's too easy to fall into the trap of treating a child as a 'safe' object for working out anger or frustration.

The truth is, of course, that, putting all other arguments against it aside for a moment, aggressive, angry or uncontrolled lashing out doesn't actually work as a form of discipline. Instead, its only lasting impact is that it's almost guaranteed to produce strained or broken relationships and children who may well be scarred for life.

For instance, if a child is constantly spanked, the emotional shock – always more lasting than the physical shock – gradually loses its impact. And once a child becomes immune, the punishment has virtually no effect on their behaviour in future. As a result, parents who use these tactics get dragged into a 'vicious circle', feeling the need to resort to even more drastic measures in order to achieve results. All this really does is turn discipline into a huge, tit-for-tat power struggle, with lots of stress, threats and heat, but no light whatsoever.

But this kind of 'undisciplined discipline' isn't just ineffective. It's also counter-productive. Rather than building up your child's trust, respect, love, confidence and self-worth, it breaks all these things down. Rather than improving your relationship with your child, it undermines and corrodes it. And eventually it will even destroy it altogether, which means that undisciplined discipline isn't just a recipe for failure. It's a recipe for absolute disaster.

Happy children usually come from families where love – which includes good, healthy discipline – forms the backbone of daily life. Good discipline produces respect and self-respect. And however painful it seems at the time, good discipline tells a child that you love them far too much to allow them to be destructive and self-destructive. It says, in effect, 'I love you too much to let you flush your life down the toilet!' So the challenge for all parents is quite simply to *dare to discipline*.

'Children aren't happy with nothing to ignore And that's what parents were created for.'

Ogden Nash

Without discipline, children won't know right from wrong

Because of the horrors of excessive punishment and undisciplined discipline, some parents now feel that *any* kind of discipline is outdated and dangerous. 'A healthy family life,' it's said, 'is all about letting kids have what they want and giving them freedom to express themselves.'

But in fact, although the idea that 'all you need is love' (as the Beatles put it) sounds reasonable enough in theory, in practice it's a disaster. The solution to *ab*use isn't *non*-use but *correct* use. Abuse of discipline, or undisciplined discipline, is a terrible thing. But having no discipline at all leads to an equal and opposite tragedy.

On a recent trip to a local supermarket, I saw both extremes demonstrated. One mum tried to keep her kids in line by swearing at them and whacking them. But the words and whallops were meaningless. They made no difference whatsoever to the children's behaviour. In the next aisle, another mum's two-year-old daughter was having a great time knocking baked bean cans on to the floor. 'Please, Charlotte darling, stop that!' her mum told her, as calmly as she could. But even though she pleaded with little Charlotte, sensitively pointing out the error of her ways, her daughter continued 'freely expressing' herself by happily knocking still more cans off the shelf. And as her mum was still gently reasoning with her, she moved on from the baked beans to the tinned tomatoes, and from there to the sweetcorn. Her mum's arguments were clear, logical, constructive, well-presented, loving . . . and ignored.

Logical persuasion by itself doesn't often work on toddlers, and there's a simple reason for this: toddlers don't think logically.

In fact, it's illogical for us to expect them to. Of course it's vital to reason with children. They must know *why* things are wrong. 'Because I said so' isn't enough. But firm disciplinary action, designed to change their behaviour, is also essential.

I recently talked to a parent whose son was totally out of control. His behaviour was no longer just embarrassing: it was now dangerous, both to himself and others. 'I can't understand it,' the parent told me. 'We gave him everything he wanted.' Unfortunately, that *was* the problem! If a child is given everything they ask for, they come to learn they can have anything they want. And the older they get, the more problems this is bound to create.

The truth is that learning to live within limits is part of what it means to be human. So if *you* don't teach your children the difference between *right* and *wrong* – and then enforce those limits – sooner or later someone else will! And it'll hurt a lot more if it happens that way than if you begin to do the job now. No parent does their child any favours by allowing them to do as they please. What's more, in the end their child is bound to resent them for not preparing them adequately for life.

In Chicago in 1924, university students Nathan Leopold and Richard Loeb killed a local schoolboy. The newspapers dubbed it 'the crime of the century'. Their trial made headlines around the world, because the two young men had no real motive for the killing. Rich, privileged and very intelligent, they'd simply come to believe they were superior to other people. They felt they were above the law, and could do anything they wanted . . . even murder. But like the rest of the world, the judge disagreed. He sentenced them to life in prison.

It's an extreme example, but it shows what can happen when kids aren't given a proper, creative framework of discipline. Kids have always pushed the boundaries, and always will. It's part of growing up, of learning what you can, and can't, do. So if these boundaries aren't clear and enforced, children simply learn that breaking them is OK.

If you don't teach your child the meaning of the word 'No' early on – when they insist, for example, that they *need* the very latest fashion in hyper-expensive trainers – then they'll assume that 'No' actually means 'Maybe', or even 'Yes'. And the more 'lines in the sand' they learn to kick over, the more difficult it becomes for them to accept any limits on their future behaviour. As parents, we must understand that if we don't say 'No' to our kids now and mean it, they'll grow up to become arrogant, obnoxious and disliked, at the very least.

> **'It is a wise father that knows his own child.'**
>
> Launcelot Gobbo in William Shakespeare's,
> *The Merchant Of Venice*

'A stitch in time . . .': don't put it off

Once, on a live phone-in show, a mum tearfully explained to me how her seventeen-year-old was totally out of control. Drink, drugs, violent and abusive behaviour . . . you name it, her child was into it. At the end of her tether, she sobbed, 'What can I do?' The tragedy was that, to a large extent, there was little she could do now except a bit of damage limitation. It was mostly too late.

It's like someone who's smoked sixty cigarettes every day of their adult life, and who's just been diagnosed as suffering from terminal lung cancer, phoning the doctor to ask what can be done to cure them. But by that stage, sadly, the doctor can't cure them. The best that can be done is to help ease the pain.

The longer you leave it to discipline your child, the harder your task becomes. The truth is that if you can't control your four-year-old, you'll never control your fourteen-year-old. Teenage years are a time of natural questioning and rebellion, but they'll be ten times worse if they're added to by a heap of unresolved problems and issues that should have been sorted out in early childhood. The critical time to win the battles over your kids' behaviour is in the early years. Don't wait until they're older, or you may find it's too late.

It's vital to start *now*, because good discipline takes a lot of thought, courage, consistency, diligence, dedication and, of course, *time*. It involves taking the time to make sure you know your child well. The parent who puts time into their task is far more likely to spot problems before they become crises. And that makes discipline not only easier, but also a lot more effective.

It's only through investing time that you can pay close enough attention to pick up on small changes in your child's behaviour and work out what the real problem is sooner rather than later. Without this, all too often what you end up doing is reacting to the 'symptom', not tackling the 'cause'.

> **'There are three ways to get something done: do it yourself, hire someone, or forbid your kids to do it.'**
>
> Marta Crane

Make sure you diagnose the situation correctly

Children misbehave in different ways and for a variety of different reasons, each needing a different course of action. That's why a parent needs to make the right diagnosis of the situation in order to make the right response.

1. **Accidents**. 'Accidents will always happen', as the saying goes. We all cause accidents. It's not just natural, it's inevitable. So don't lay into your kids for their accidents – they probably feel bad enough already. For instance, if your son breaks a window while playing football in the back garden, however frustrating or annoying it may be, it's probably just an accident. Don't react. Think about it. You sent them to play in the garden, and probably even

bought them the ball for that very purpose. You just didn't reckon on how far or hard they could kick it! (Of course, if you specifically told them *not* to play football in the garden, that's a different matter, and should be dealt with in a different way. What's important then is that you punish them for their disobedience, not for breaking the window as such. Though it's an immediate problem, very annoying and expensive to replace, the window is still relatively unimportant, believe me! But if you don't tackle the issue of their disobedience now, it'll lead to much bigger trouble later on.)

2. **Mistakes**. These are really shortsighted judgments or bad decisions that result from a lack of wisdom. We all make them, though with experience we hopefully make fewer and fewer. Like accidents, mistakes aren't deliberate. Last month, for instance, one of my sons accidentally left his clarinet on the bus. It took him a full week to tell us he'd lost it, which was a silly mistake. I understand why he did it: it was a kind of head-in-the-sand manoeuvre. But if he'd told us about it on the day it happened, we could have phoned up the bus company and had it back the next day, and he wouldn't have been punished. But because he left it a week, we decided to dock his pocket money. He needed to learn to be more responsible in his care of very valuable possessions. When we explained this to him, he agreed this punishment was fair, even though he didn't like it. And hopefully he won't bury his head in the sand again in quite the same way.

3. **Cries For Help**. What seems like lack of discipline can sometimes be a cry for help. When your two-year-old cries at bedtime every night, for example, are they trying to get their own way or are they genuinely afraid of the dark? When your first child misbehaves or rebels after the arrival of a new baby in the family, is it really a cry for attention because they need to know you still love them?

Is your twelve-year-old's sudden lack of interest in school actually the result of being bullied, or feeling unable to cope? It takes time and care to find out. And just as a doctor doesn't take one glance at a patient and then simply *guess* at what the problem is, so a wise parent doesn't jump too hastily to conclusions either. They're concerned enough to take time to find out *why* their child is behaving as they are.

4. **Challenges**. These are far more serious. They are deliberate acts of rebellion. Every child sometimes pushes the boundaries to see where they are and, more importantly, how firmly they're fixed. This is nothing less than a throwing down of the gauntlet – a challenge to a duel. *It's absolutely vital that you meet these challenges head-on and win them.* You can't afford not to, or they'll come back to haunt you later, when they'll be much harder to win. If you can't make a five-year-old pick up her toys when you ask, what chance do you have with a teenager? If you're too weak or too tired or too busy to win, there's big trouble ahead. All cold-blooded challenges must be faced. Maintaining your authority is a key part of winning your child's respect. And remember: winning the duel is the act of a loving parent, even if your child doesn't react by wanting to cuddle you for it straight afterwards!

> **'Give yourself an hour to cool off before responding to someone who has provoked you.'**
>
> H. Jackson Brown, Jnr

Make the punishment fit the crime

So how *should* a parent discipline their child?

No punishment or discipline does any good if it's arbitrary – handed out because of the mood a parent happens to be in at the time – or if it's carried out in the heat of the moment. That's why it's always a good idea to have a short 'cooling off period' before taking any action, even if (in the case of young children) it's only a couple of minutes. This gives you the time you need to get control of yourself, assess the situation and think about what your response will be before you hand out a suitable punishment. It might even give your child time to reflect on what they've done wrong, and calm down or apologise.

It's too easy simply to lash out and punish a child in the heat of the moment, and then regret it later on – or worse still, not regret it when you should have. This kind of discipline is undisciplined, and therefore useless for teaching your kids any contructive lessons except to stay out of your way! Instead, stop, cool down, think, plan and *then* act.

It's only when you stop and think first that you're in a fit state to act and make a good choice of punishment: one that's appropriate not just to the 'crime', but also to the child who's committed it. That's because being fair in your treatment of kids doesn't necessarily mean doling out the same punishment to every child who commits the same offence. Children react in different ways. A sensitive child, for example, may learn their lesson just from a firm talking to, without any need for further action. So sending them to their room would be overkill.

Remember that vengeance should never be the goal of punishment. Its aim is, rather, to reinforce the boundaries your children have broken, letting them know that the limits of acceptable behaviour really can't be broken. So the only valid reason for punishing your kids is not to destroy them, but to build them up and equip them for life.

In the famous chariot scene from the film *Ben Hur*, Joshua Ben Hur has to race a team of four powerful stallions at full speed around Rome's Circus Maximus stadium. Driving these wild horses in a straight line and getting them to work together round the corners without overturning the chariot takes real skill. If Ben Hur allows them to slow down, he'll lose the race:

he needs their energy to win. But if he doesn't harness that energy, then chariot, horses and rider will all go crashing into the barriers and out of the race.

A parent has the same kind of task as Ben Hur. Punishment, like good discipline in general, should never be used to break a child's spirit and energy, but always to harness and guide it constructively rather than destructively. So all punishment should be:

- **Fair**. If a punishment isn't fair, your child will learn nothing about self-control and responsibility from it. What they *will* learn is that you're not fair. As a result, they'll feel angry, rejected, and misunderstood – all emotions guaranteed to produce more bad behaviour in future. By taking a short cut, not thinking, and being unfair in the punishment you hand out, you'll only end up adding to your problems and giving yourself a much bigger battle to fight later on . . . by which time they'll respect and trust you a lot less.

- **Firm**. Make sure your 'No' means no and your 'Yes' means yes. Don't make idle threats. If you mean 'No', say it and stick to it, or all you'll teach your kids is that they can get whatever they want, so long as they're prepared to grind you down for long enough. In other words, they'll end up believing that tantrums and other forms of disobedience work provided they are dedicated and persevere long enough to get their own way. So choose your battles carefully, and make sure you stand your ground when it matters.

- **Consistent**. Don't allow your moods to influence your decisions about punishment. If something is wrong, it's wrong, however tired you are. The boundaries must always be there. If an offence is treated as trivial one week and serious the next, your child will end up confused about where and what the boundaries really are.

'Reasoning with a child is fine, if you can reach the child's reason without destroying your own.'

John Mason Brown

To smack or not to smack?

Smacking is a big issue. An American expert was explaining on British TV why she thought smacking was a terrible 'violation of basic human rights', and likely to leave a child needing therapy. 'We've got to *talk* out the problems instead,' she concluded. But her interviewer was unconvinced: 'Perhaps a good smack is the right therapy sometimes,' she quipped.

So who's right? Is smacking a form of punishment whose time is past? Does it scar kids emotionally for life and teach them that violence is the way to solve their problems? Or can it have a positive effect, helping to give them the self-respect and self-discipline they need?

Every parent will make up their own mind about whether or not – and in what circumstances – it's right to smack their child. But as they do, they need to think long and hard about the issues involved and alternatives available.

To begin with, a disciplined parent won't always want to use the same form of punishment. They'll want to choose a punishment that fits both the 'crime' and the child – and there's lots of scope for creativity here. In fact, alternative punishments to smacking fall into three basic categories:

- **Withdrawing privileges** – including the removal of pocket money or treats, not being allowed to stay up late at weekends, limiting the use of computers or other toys, banning of favourite TV programmes, grounding, and other restrictions.
- **Sending children to a 'cooling off' place** – e.g. their bedroom or a corner of the room. (However, if you do this, make sure that it's a real punishment: a friend of mine

loved being sent to his room, where he could do what he wanted without being seen!) A couple I know send their kids half-way up the stairs for half an hour whenever they're naughty. They say it's effective because there's nothing for them to do there except think about what they did wrong.

- **Verbal tellings-off** – a serious talk in a serious voice will sometimes have the desired effect. Your kids want you to be pleased with them, so letting them know they've disappointed you can be extremely effective.

There are some people who claim that smacking is wrong because, unlike other forms of punishment, it's violent and abusive. But the truth is that when a parent shouts and screams uncontrollably at their child, or sends them to their room while they're in a furious temper, or stops their pocket money as part of an unthought-out and angry reaction to a mistake, this is every bit as 'violent', abusive and emotionally scarring as an uncaring smack or slap.

A few years ago, the director of one infamous children's home was sacked not just for beating the children in his care, but equally for using a system known as 'pin-down', where he confined them to their rooms for days at a time.

The problem, in other words, isn't really about smacking as such. It's deeper than that. It's about the way in which a punishment – *any* punishment – is given. There's a world of difference between tapping a toddler lightly on the wrist and giving a child an angry or prolonged thrashing with a hand or belt. In fact, lumping these together under one label – 'smacking' – as if they were all the same, is extremely misleading.

The truth is that *any* punishment given to a child as an unthought-out, arbitrary or violent reaction is abusive. And that doesn't just apply to smacking. It's exactly the same for sending a child to their room, withdrawing their pocket money, shouting at them or anything else. Any punishment that's undisciplined and handed out in the heat of the moment is bound to be damaging. It's this kind of punishment that will confuse and scar a child emotionally . . . and, of course, won't work anyway. But the double tragedy with out-of-control smacking is that the already devastating impact of emotional scarring and damage caused by undisciplined discipline is added to by physical pain and abuse.

> **'It's as easy to make someone feel reassured and good as it is to destroy that person.'**
> Eleanore Phillips Colt

Always end positively

The last word, after any punishment, must always be a positive one. It's very important for your children to know they've done wrong. But it's every bit as important for them to know that you love them anyway. So always make sure you let them know that the only reason you're punishing them is because you love them. Otherwise they may think that you like punishing them, or that you only love them when they're being good. And that, of course, is never the message you want to send.

DAD'S TWO-HOUR EXPLANATIONS OF WHY PUNISHMENT IS BEING GIVEN ARE WORSE THAN THE PUNISHMENTS THEMSELVES.

My dad had a favourite phrase that he often used when he had to punish me: 'This hurts me a lot more than it hurts you!' And not surprisingly, like every other kid who's ever heard those words, I didn't believe them. But as I've grown older and had children of my own, I've come to see that he was telling the truth. It's painful to punish your children. A good parent will agonise over the punishment, but still feel compelled to act rather than turn a blind eye. The reason is simply that they love their child too much to let them get away with doing something wrong and destructive without learning that it is wrong and destructive. So love and discipline your children . . . just don't expect them to jump for joy and thank you for it at the time!

Remember

- Discipline is about a lot more than punishment. It's about giving your child the best start in life you can.
- Love isn't the opposite of discipline – it's the reason for it.
- Discipline doesn't restrict freedom – it creates it.
- Punishment is just one small part of good discipline.
- 'Undisciplined discipline' and no discipline are both recipes for disaster.
- If you can't control your three-year-old, you'll never control them when they're thirteen.
- Good discipline is the result of investing time.
- A punishment needs to fit both the crime and the child who's committed it.

Key principles

Always be disciplined in the way you discipline your kids.

How to achieve it

- Don't just lash out. Stop and think before 'passing sentence'.
- Think about the effect your punishment will have, not just whether you think it's justified or not.
- Always explain why a punishment is being given.
- Always reassure your kids that you love them *after* you've punished them.

Be Encouraging

Praise your children for what they do right

'Fatherhood is . . . pretending that the present you love most is soap-on-a-rope.'

Bill Cosby

Discipline gives children a moral reference point

'Teach a child where they should go, and when they're old they'll keep on down that path.' Good advice from an old proverb in the Bible. The reason we discipline our kids is in order to create a sense of self-discipline in their lives. Self-discipline acts like an internal gyroscope, helping them to control their own behaviour and order their lives constructively. And when they're grown up and you're not there any more, it'll give them the ability to keep a level head even if everything around them is threatening to throw them off balance.

Until the mid-eighteenth century, sailing around the world was extremely hazardous. Sensible globe-trotting mariners would sail along a country's coastline whenever they could rather than risk the open sea, because there was no way to tell accurately where you were once you'd left the safety of land. But all that changed in 1759, when clockmaker John Harrison invented the 'maritime chronometer'. With a chronometer, it was possible for the first time to pin-point your exact position wherever you were in the world by comparing it to Greenwich, which acted as a reference point.

And that meant that you wouldn't get lost any more.

Parents who carefully, lovingly and often painstakingly discipline their children are actually helping them develop a kind of 'moral chronometer'. So wherever they go and whatever they do later in life, they'll be able to trust their judgment and make good decisions by using their childhood as a reliable reference point.

You can't hide your kids from life's storms. They're going to have to face them head on sooner or later, just like everyone else. The only real question is how well equipped they will be to cope when it happens – and that's the bit that's up to you. Through the use of thoughtful and loving discipline *now*, you can create that vital reference point for them in the years ahead.

> **'The best way to keep children is to make the home atmosphere pleasant – and let the air out of the tyres.'**
>
> Dorothy Parker

The right tool for the right job

In 1912, the famous ship, the *Titanic*, sank on its maiden voyage from Liverpool to New York. Dubbed 'unsinkable', this gigantic floating hotel plummeted to the bottom of the Atlantic Ocean with the loss of 1,500 lives after hitting a massive iceberg. But the interesting thing is that the iceberg did most of its damage *underneath* the water's surface, gouging a massive hole out of the side of the ship and allowing water in at an astonishing rate. In fact, it's reckoned that around 90 per cent of any iceberg is invisible, always hidden beneath the ocean waves. Only the tip – the top 10 per cent – ever floats above the water line.

Punishment has a part to play in good discipline. But the truth is that, though it tends to be the part that gets seen and talked about the most, it's only the tip of the iceberg. Because punishment is the most obvious form of discipline, many parents act as if that's all there is to it. So we pull our kids up and penalise them over everything they do wrong, but never think (or somehow forget) to encourage them about all the things they do right. And then we wonder why they struggle to develop the self-confidence we want them to have.

MY KIDS HAVE JUST PRAISED ME FOR BEING GOOD AT GIVING PRAISE!

There's a lot more to discipline than punishment, and that's what this chapter is all about. Praise, encouragement, thanks, listening and respect are like the other 90 per cent of the iceberg that never gets seen. They form the basis on which your child's self-esteem and self-discipline are built, and without them, all the punishment in the world will do no good, and an awful lot of harm. It's not a question of either/or: *either* punishing your kids *or* praising them. It's more a case of both/ and: in order to be effective, good discipline requires the use of *both* appropriate punishment (teaching your children when they've done something wrong) *and* praise (teaching them when they've done something right).

In the cupboard under the stairs in our house is a big metal box filled with lots of tools. When Cornelia and I first got married, this box was a lot smaller and virtually empty. But gradually the number of tools it contained grew as I found I never had the right tool to do the job that needed doing around the house. So over the years, I've added an assorted collection of spanners, sockets, hack-saws, Allen keys, tape measures, screwdrivers, chisels, pliers, wrenches and a spirit level. I may not be 'Mr DIY', but even I know that you can't fix everything with a hammer!

And discipline is exactly the same. You can't do the whole job with just one tool . . . especially if it's a hammer! So a wise parent is one who understands the need to use a wide variety of disciplinary tools and sensitively chooses the right one from their tool kit for each occasion. And though appropriate punishment is one of these tools, it's *only* one. And in the normal run of things, there are a great many others that a parent would do well to reach for more frequently.

> **'The task of leadership is not to put greatness into people, but to draw it out.'**
>
> John Buchan

Love is the most durable power in the world

Everyone knows that there are two very different ways to get a dog to obey you. You can either choose to beat it into submission, or to build a relationship with it based on mutual trust and respect. Of course, it's vital to discipline your dog and teach it to obey your commands, and being firm is an essential part of this. But unless you're loving as well, it will never respond to you with enthusiasm, and you'll never know what it means to be able to call your dog 'man's (or woman's) best friend'.

It was Mao Tse Tung, the former Chinese leader, who said, 'Power grows out of the barrel of a gun.' As far as he was concerned, fear was the most reliable way of ensuring that you got what you wanted from people. They would do whatever you told them to if they were sufficiently afraid of the consequences of *not* doing it. But another world leader, Martin Luther King, had a very different approach to things. He taught that love was considerably more powerful than fear. In fact, he called love 'the most durable power in the world'. And ultimately, every parent has to decide whether to copy the style of Mao Tse Tung or Martin Luther King.

Your child's long-term emotional stability depends on whether or not they feel loved and valued *now*. An adult's self-esteem grows out of the knowledge that they're unique and valuable. Your children will inevitably be exposed to all sorts of pressure throughout their lives. But if, in their early years, you've built into them an assurance that they're loved and valued, they'll not only survive, they'll go on to thrive.

It's every parent's task to love their children for *who they are* (with no strings attached), and for most parents, of course, that's not a hard thing to do ... it comes naturally. Their love for their children is instinctive. But it's also very important for parents to praise their children for *what they do*, because praise reinforces love. It shows kids what they're good at and what's special about them. And this makes it easier for them to believe their parents love them.

If you think you're not good for anything, it's hard to believe someone when they say they love you. You can't understand

I'D LIKE TO PRAISE YOU FOR HAVING THE GOOD SENSE TO TAKE YOUR LOOKS FROM ME AND NOT YOUR FATHER...

why they should love you, because you can't see anything of value in yourself. This is why praise is so important to your children. It shows them what's *right* with them. And it's why it's an essential tool for helping build up the self-esteem they need to be happy. Children who know how valuable they are can survive the ups and downs of life. But if they don't know this, sooner or later they may well buckle under the pressure.

> **'When you are young, every small thing is make or break.'**
>
> Mary Quant

The management technique of nagging and yelling

Give a good idea to an American, and by the time you've finished telling them about it they'll have come up with three reasons why it's the best idea they've ever heard. Explain the same idea to a Brit, and by the time you've finished they'll have come up with three reasons why it'll never work! It's part of who we are. We tend not to be very good at giving praise. And we're not used to accepting it. So we assume that our kids somehow *know* that we love them, and know what's good about them, even though we never actually tell them.

How often have you heard someone say something like, 'They don't really appreciate me' or, 'My boss just doesn't value me'? I hear this kind of complaint all the time. But in ninety-nine cases out of a hundred, I know it's not true. In fact, quite often the reason why I'm so sure that their friends, colleagues or bosses know how valuable and important they are is because they've told me so outright. It's just that they never thought to tell the person in question. We all assume that people who never *tell* us they appreciate us, *don't* appreciate us. And your children are no different.

So why aren't we more honest and open with our praise and encouragement? There are three reasons:

- We're not in the habit.
- We're afraid of looking or feeling silly and vulnerable.
- We're afraid that it will turn our children into big-headed monsters!

The irony of all this is that praise is actually productive. A friend of mine talks about the management technique of 'nagging and yelling'. No one with any sense would run a business the way some people run their families, he says. If they did, pretty soon they wouldn't have a business left to run. And it's true. Over the last fifteen years, more and more business leaders have come to realise that praise is profitable.

When you yell at people or nag them to get things done, all you do is gradually eat away at their enthusiasm for their job. And eventually they'll come to resent it, and you, so much that you'll get nothing more than the bare minimum out of them. But if you learn to praise people for the good work they do, they start to feel good about themselves and want to achieve more. Their confidence grows, and as a result they do an even better job.

I've found exactly the same thing in my job as the director of a charity. Even when people let me down, bawling them out is one of the worst possible ways of getting them to learn from their mistakes and do better in the future. Shouting, 'Why wasn't this done? It's just not good enough' demotivates people rather than inspiring them. It's far more effective to highlight the positive things about them, praising and encouraging them for the things they've done well, and then to raise any negative things within that context. Praise helps people recognise and build on what they *can* do, working hard to overcome their weaknesses. Criticism only makes them feel bad about what they *can't* do, encouraging them just to give up.

And what's true for the workplace is just as true for the family. Like all great truths, it seems blindingly obvious once you stop to think about it. It's simply a case of 'reaping what you sow'. If you praise your children for what they do well and do right, they'll not only feel good about themselves and understand their strengths, they'll also work hard at building on them.

We used to live in a London borough where our local council was convinced that competition was unhelpful and negative. In fact, my son's school had banned all competitive sports. One Saturday, when he was about eight, we were walking together through the local park and happened to stumble across a football match. He was amazed to see boys his own age dressed in kit, and playing in teams on a real pitch with a referee. He stood and watched for a while and then asked me where the TV cameras were. I laughed, it seemed like such a daft question. It was only later that I realised that the only real football matches he knew about were *professional* ones on the TV. He had no idea that other schoolboys or anyone else played real matches in real kit, just for fun!

Trying to protect children from competition is more than just shortsighted. It's stupid, and ultimately doomed to failure. Sooner or later, every child has to deal both with competition and with not always winning. Part of a parent's job is to help their children learn how to cope with failure, rather than pretending that the world isn't really like that. So if you regularly praise your son or daughter for the things they do well, it'll help them to see their failures and weaknesses in context. It will help them learn how to face up to, and cope with, their limitations while concentrating on their strengths. If everything you do seems to be wrong, then 'losing' can be a devastating blow. But when you know you're good at something else, failure is a lot easier to deal with.

When my elder daughter was at school she was well aware that her greatest gift in life was not on the sports field. But this wasn't something she found devastating to come to terms with, because she also knew that she was excellent at languages. In fact, she was the only fifteen-year-old I've ever known who not only understood, but actually *enjoyed*, Shakespeare. *I* used to hate it! Cornelia and I have tried hard to encourage her in the things she likes and the things she's good at. And as a result of knowing her strengths, I hope she's learning more easily to accept her weaknesses.

> **'The days that make us happy make us wise.'**
> John Masefield

Praise is the miracle tool

Children, like adults, do their best when they feel good about themselves. And they feel good about themselves when they're *told* they're doing well. There's an almost automatic connection. In 1904, Ivan Pavlov was awarded the Nobel Prize for Medicine for his work on what we now call 'conditioned responses'. He discovered that if he rang a bell when he fed his dog, the dog associated the bell with food. After a while, whenever he rang the bell, the dog turned up *expecting* food. Like it or not, the truth is that we humans react in much the same way. We make choices, of course, but we also make mental 'associations' and act accordingly.

So when Luciano Pavarotti performed in London a few years ago, the audience surprised him by trying to sing along to one of the songs on the programme. But while Pavarotti sang 'O Sole Mio', the audience chanted 'Just One Cornetto'. TV adverts from years before had firmly linked the old tune with ice cream. And 'O Sole Mio' wasn't the only song to strike a chord. 'Nessun Dorma', from Puccini's opera *Turandot*, was just as well known because it was the theme tune to the 1990 World Cup.

We all understand the power of a negative mental 'association'. That's why we punish our children for doing something bad. We're relying on them associating their punishment with their 'crime'. We hope it'll make them think twice next time. But positive associations are just as important. Your kids *want* to feel valued and appreciated. So if you praise them when they do something right, they'll be more likely to do it again. And if you praise them for putting in the effort, they'll want to try just as hard, if not harder, in the future.

Just as a flower blossoms when you give it enough water, and dies when you neglect it, so your child's self-confidence will bloom when you praise them and wither when you don't. Experts call this the Law of Reinforcement – 'behaviour which achieves desirable consequences will recur' – but to most of us it just seems like plain, old-fashioned common sense.

Most human behaviour is learned. We learn how to play the piano or play tennis in just the same way that we learn to fight, bully, whine or throw temper tantrums. We avoid actions we know have bad consequences, and repeat actions that seem to be successful. A toddler won't hesitate to throw a tantrum in the middle of a crowded supermarket if they know from past experience that it'll get them what they want. In the same way, Friday, our cat, always wakes me up first thing in the morning by miaowing and scratching at the bedroom door. He knows I'll eventually get so sick of the noise that I'll get up and let him out. And though I hate to admit it, I know that every time I give in and do it, I reinforce his habit and make the chances of ever getting a lie-in even slimmer.

And it works for positive things too. So if you want your kids to go to the toilet by themselves, clean their teeth, pick up their clothes, do their homework, tidy their rooms, work hard, tell the truth, be generous, be polite and courteous, or think of others, then praise is by far the most effective way to achieve it. Because if they like what happens when they do something, they'll do it again.

The golden rule is this: *catch your kids red-handed doing something right . . . and praise them for it!*

WELL DONE FOR
GIVING ME SO MANY
THINGS TO PRAISE
YOU
FOR...

'One of the horribly character-forming things about life [is that] praise is least forthcoming from the people who know us best, and love us most.'

Craig Brown, *Evening Standard*

How NOT to praise your children

So praise your children frequently. But as you do so, be careful to steer clear of the following common pitfalls:

1. **Avoid Fake Praise**: Don't ever allow your desire to praise your kids push you into lying to them. Insincere praise won't help them. It's patronising, and has the effect of completely devaluing any genuine praise you offer them on other occasions.
2. **Avoid Vague Praise**: Always be specific in your praise. That way, your children will know *exactly* what they did right, and will begin to recognise their strengths. So don't just say, 'That was good'. Be specific, and explain *why* it was good: 'That was clever/thoughtful/kind/sensitive/ brave/helpful/imaginative' or 'You tried hard, well done'.

3. **Avoid Achievement-Related Praise**: Praise your
    children for the skill and effort they've put into an
    achievement, not for the achievement itself. If you praise
    them for what they've achieved, they will begin to link
    your approval and love with their success, not their
    effort. As a result, the self-esteem you're trying to
    establish will be destroyed. So praise the *deed* rather than
    the *person*, and the *process* rather than the *product*. Praise
    them for their effort, their choices, their thoughtfulness,
    their independence, their skills, their helpfulness, or their
    ideas, not for their success.

4. **Avoid Qualified Praise**: Praise your child for their
    effort and stop there. Don't make the mistake of
    following it up with a fifteen-minute lecture on how they
    could have done *even better* if only they'd have . . . For
    example, if your son proudly shows you the Lego space
    ship it's taken him three hours to build, resist the
    temptation to add bits to it or tell him how he can
    improve it. Instead, be enthusiastic with him about what
    he's achieved. Because even if the finely-engineered,
    fully-functioning scale model of the Starship Enterprise
    you'd like to turn it into is more impressive than his
    original creation, it'll no longer be *his*. By telling your
    kids how to improve things, what you actually do is send
    them the message that their effort isn't quite good
    enough for you. All they'll remember is the criticism, not
    the praise. (In fact, experts reckon it takes eighteen
    pieces of praise to counteract the effects of just *one* piece
    of negative criticism!) So encourage your children to do
    better simply by praising them for their hard work and
    effort. That way, they'll know what strengths they have to
    build on, and they'll have the enthusiasm to do it.

5. **Avoid Comparative Praise**: Always tell your child,
    'You did well.' Never say, 'You were better than so and
    so.' Above all, don't praise them for being 'the best'. The

comparison that really matters is with their own past performance. If they did *their* best, that's what counts. Whether they did better or worse than someone else is irrelevant. You'll do your child a big favour if you help them to measure their effort against *their* standards, not someone else's.

6. **Avoid Manipulative Praise**: Believe it or not, not all praise is good. Sometimes we can fall into the trap of praising people to 'warm them up', so we can then ask them for a favour. 'That's great, love . . . Now get us a cup of tea, will you?' is just a way of buttering someone up in order to get what you want out of them. So even if your praise is entirely authentic, don't connect it with a request. It'll make it seem insincere. And if you're insincere on one occasion, how is your child supposed to know if you're being genuine on another?

7. **Avoid Material Praise**: Resist the temptation to give material incentives: 'If you do well in your GCSEs, I'll get you that bike you wanted.' If they fail, you'll find yourself having to be firm and withholding a present at just the time they need to feel your love and acceptance the most. And the situation's not much better if they succeed. A friend of mine, Jill, always used to hate the incentive prizes her father dangled in front of her to do well at school. 'If something was worth doing,' she says, 'I figured it was worth doing anyway. When Dad had to offer me an incentive to do something, it was like saying it wasn't really worth doing in the first place. So why bother? It would have meant so much more if he'd just given me the present because he *wanted* to.' If you want to give your child a gift, give it, being careful not to spoil them. But never use treats as incentives.

Remember

- Healthy discipline creates self-discipline and self-esteem.
- Healthy discipline gives your children a moral reference point for the future.
- Praise and encouragement are essential tools for healthy discipline.
- Praise tells children they're valuable and lets them feel loved.
- Praising kids for what they do right gives them motivation to build on their strengths and the confidence to cope with their weaknesses.
- Kids like being praised, so they'll keep doing things you praise them for.
- Praise should always be sincere, or it'll do more harm than good.

Key principles

Catch your children red-handed doing something right, and praise them for it.

How to achieve it

- Praise your kids for the effort they put in, not for being the best.
- Praise them enthusiastically. Don't be half-hearted.
- Don't be general in your praise. Be specific.
- Make sure you send your children more positive messages than negative ones.

Be Careful

Remember you're a role model

> 'You're kind of a father figure to me, dad.'
>
> Alan Coren

Parents lay the foundations of their kids' lives

In 1994, six months after a devastating earthquake, I visited Maharashtra State in India. More than 25,000 people had lost their lives in just forty seconds. The damage was almost unbelievable. In one village, every house was totally demolished except for one, which didn't even have a single crack in the plaster. It belonged to a rich man. And in a village built basically of stones, mud and wood, his was the only home made from bricks and mortar on a proper foundation. Had all the houses in the sixty-six towns and villages destroyed been built like this one, no one would have lost their life.

Foundations are vital. Without them, you're in big trouble. And childhood is the foundation for the rest of life. Whatever we build on top will only survive if the foundation is deep enough and strong enough to support it. It's we parents who lay the foundations of our children's lives. Without doubt, the main responsibility for producing mature, independent, well-motivated, creative, adult members of society belongs not to the school, media or wider society – though all these undoubtedly help or hinder – but to parents. The buck stops here!

School isn't an Adult Machine. It's not a factory that takes young children and processes them into fresh, vibrant, productive members of the community. Neither are the Boy Scouts, Girl Guides, Army Training Corps, Sunday School, snooker hall, football club, Youth Hostels Association, Cake Bake Club or the Margaret Whiffle Academy For Young Ladies. Parents can't abdicate their responsibility to any other group, however helpful a job they do. All of these institutions can play an important role working in partnership with the family, but no one else can do a parent's job. And no one else should.

As the saying goes, 'Fish rots from the head down'. This morning, I was listening to *Today* on Radio 4. A mother explained what she'd learnt from a parenting course. 'I was always going down to the school to stick up for my Philip,' she said. 'The teachers said he was unteachable and a troublemaker. But I wasn't having any of that! I used to get mad. It wasn't Philip's fault. He was being set up . . . provoked. But the thing is, he's so different now. Ever since I went on the parent course, I've felt in control. And Philip's behaviour has been transformed. I now realise that his problems were never really *his* problems. They were mine.'

> **'Gentlemen, these are my principles. But if you don't like them, I've got other ones.'**
>
> Cecil B. de Mille

Your kids are under the influence of somebody all the time

We've all heard about identical twins, separated at birth, who've got the same taste in food, clothes, music and even the opposite sex. It seems that our genes play an important part in determining the kind of person we turn out to be. But having said that, it's undoubtedly true that our character is also shaped by our influences, our choices and our upbringing, which is why we've also heard of identical twins, separated at birth, who turn out to have completely different tastes in music, fashion, friends and just about everything else.

In other words, 'nature' and 'nurture' *both* play a part in deciding who we are and what we're like as people. Now you can't do anything about your children's genes. He or she got them from you and is stuck with them (which is at least one good reason for being tolerant of their shortcomings). But you *can* do lots to influence their personality by being careful about how you bring them up.

One of the greatest gifts any parent can give their child, to help equip them for life, is a value system. Some parents are worried about imposing their morals on their kids. They're afraid of over-influencing or even brainwashing them. But the truth is that everyone else is interested in influencing your children's values even if you're not. They're being bombarded by a huge array of influences all the time. Even the old idea that children could be given a 'value-free' education at school is dead and buried. Something of the teacher's own values will always creep in.

Several years ago, I went to South Africa to make a TV programme. One of the people I had to interview for the programme was Dr Bayers Naudé. Winner of the Nobel Peace Prize, he'd been a fierce opponent of apartheid for more than twenty-five years. But many years ago, as a young man training to be a priest, he'd genuinely believed that apartheid was 'God's will for South Africa'. It's what he'd been taught as a boy. It's what all his friends and colleagues believed. Even though he was an extremely clever man, he'd never thought to question it. 'Apartheid was simply taken for granted,' he said.

So the question isn't, 'Are your kids being brainwashed?' It's 'What are your kids' brains being washed with?' Children are like sponges: they'll soak up their values from somewhere. So if *you* don't influence them, someone else *will*. In fact, if you're not influencing your kids, you're about the only person in their life who isn't. Someone else is doing it for you, only with *their* values and *their* standards, not *yours*. But if your children are going to be influenced by someone, it might as well be you. And if you're not sure that your values are worth passing on, then change them *now*! Because if they're not worth passing on, they're not worth having.

Your kids are constantly bombarded by different opinions on all sorts of subjects: sex, drugs, music, politics, the environment, money, fashion, religion, war, animal rights, homosexuality, careers, food, art, transport, race, gender, language, sport . . . the list is endless. Some of these opinions are just other people's opinions. But some are deliberate attempts to persuade your kids that a particular view is the one they *should* have. Rightly or wrongly, there's a real battle going on for your child's mind (and money).

The experts tell us that the average dad spends just three minutes a day in 'quality' conversation with his kids. The average mum does slightly better, knocking up five and a half minutes. By contrast, the average child spends three hours a day watching TV. In fact, some kids have TVs in their bedrooms, and many sitting-rooms are arranged around the TV just like a mini-cinema. The only things some families seem to do together are eat and watch television, and even eating is often done in front of the TV.

YOU NEED TO THINK FOR YOURSELF, JON — AT LEAST THAT'S WHAT I'VE LEARNED FROM THE TELLY...

So it doesn't take Einstein to work out who has the major influence on many kids' lives. Their values, morals and beliefs are all shaped by what they see on TV. But they're also constantly influenced by school, music, magazines, computers, radio, advertising, books, videos, other adults, pressure groups, friends and even friends' parents. In fact, your kids are exposed to an overwhelming barrage of views and values every day of their lives.

Of course, you can and should restrict the influences your children are exposed to. It's part of a parent's responsibility carefully to monitor what their kids watch on TV, see at the cinema or read in books and magazines, as well as where they go with their friends, etc. But none of this can ever produce a totally 'bad-influence-free' environment for them to live in. Whatever you do, you can't stop your child being influenced by all sorts of views and opinions, however hard you try. So your *real* job is to help them understand and cope with these conflicting opinions better. And the best way of doing that, for instance, is to talk to them about the issues they see on TV, rather than pretending they haven't been raised.

Several years ago, my friend Claire was so concerned about the values being peddled by one of the TV soaps that she banned her kids from watching it. But the plan backfired. Her children ended up feeling like outcasts at school, since everyone else had seen the show the night before. What's more, they weren't even being 'protected' from the values it presented. They were just hearing them second-hand – sometimes consider-ably amplified for effect! So instead, Claire began watching it with them so that they could occasionally chat about the programme, the characters and their behaviour. Then at least the show's values were no longer entering their awareness unfiltered.

Your kids are at the beginning of their lives. It's as though they're just setting sail on a life-long voyage. But as yet their rudder doesn't guide them too well. They don't yet know how to make mature and sensible decisions or how to understand all the opinions that bombard them. So it's your job to help them steer. It's your responsibility to stand at the helm with them, guiding and advising them as they turn the rudder. And this isn't just a duty, it's also a wonderful and extremely exciting privilege. So don't miss out on it.

> **'One day you look in the mirror and realise that the face you are shaving is your father's.'**
>
> Robert Harris

Like it or not, children become like their parents

How many parents have wished revenge on their naughty children with the words: 'When you grow up, I hope you have kids just like you'? The irony is, of course, that this wish will come true. Like it or not, *all* kids turn into partial copies of their parents, because all parents influence their children, whether intentionally or not.

A few generations ago, the older girls in most homes would become their mother's informal assistants, learning to help care for the younger children in the family, which is where the term 'mother's little helper' comes from. Meanwhile, their brothers learnt their father's trade alongside him. If their dad was a carpenter or blacksmith, they'd follow in his footsteps and become a carpenter or blacksmith themselves. But parents passed on far more than just their skills. Slowly and surely, through the time they spent with their children, they passed on their values as well. As children worked beside their mum or dad, they learnt about the whole of life . . . even how to be a parent! And for the most part, it was all achieved without lectures or pressure – these lessons were learnt by example.

I once met a man, now in his late eighties, who complained that he just couldn't understand 'today's young people'. 'When I was fourteen,' he told me, 'all I wanted to be was like my dad . . . and to have a suit like his.' He looked up to his father and respected him enormously. He couldn't think of anything better than to be just like him . . . even down to his taste in clothing.

Times have changed. But it's still true that during the first years of their lives, your children actively *want* to copy what you do and say. You're their hero, and they want to be like you. Nothing matters more to them than what you think. And although this time will pass, what they learn from you during it will play a vital part in forming the foundations on which their personality and whole approach to life will be built. If you're honest and kind, they're likely to be honest and kind. If you're rude and arrogant, they're likely to be rude and arrogant. If you're lazy, they may well end up just like you. If you sleep around, they'll sleep around. And if you use violence and bullying to get your way, they'll use violence and bullying to get their way. That's a very powerful position to be in. So it's vitally important that you get it right.

IS YOUR DAD A ROLE MODEL?

YEAH – NEVER 'ROLES' OUT OF BED BEFORE LUNCHTIME ON SUNDAY.

'**Fathers should not get too discouraged if their sons reject their advice. It will not be wasted; years later the sons will offer it to their own offspring.**'

Anonymous

'Do as I say, not as I do'

But how *do* you pass on the right values? Well, the first thing to say is that it doesn't happen overnight. You can't sit your kids down for a mammoth, six-hour, 'Big Value' talk and hope that'll do the trick. It takes a long time. At least fourteen years, in fact! It's a slow process, like filling a bath from a dripping tap.

So start NOW! And remember, values are both *caught* and *taught*.

1. **Values are Caught**. Many of your values are passed on *accidentally*. From long before the time they're able to make 'value judgments', your kids will copy what you say and do, both consciously and unconsciously. Just as they'll adopt your gestures and mannerisms, they'll also swallow your values. So if you don't want your child to learn something from you, don't do it. The old adage, 'Do as I say, not as I do,' never works. Whatever you tell your kids about your values, they'll check to see how it all works out in practice in your life. For instance, it's no use trying to teach your kids about honesty if you then ask them to lie and say you're not in to answer the phone when you are. And it's no good teaching them to do their homework every night if all they ever see you do in the evenings is slob out in front of the TV. (Besides everything else, it's incredibly hard to concentrate when you know that everyone else is downstairs doing nothing!) If you try to teach your kids values you don't actually live by, they'll know it. And they'll slowly come

to an obvious conclusion: you're a hypocrite. Then they'll probably reject your values, and maybe even you as well. So get your act up to scratch. If you want them to do it, make sure they see *you* doing it. And remember, the values your children catch from you will probably eventually be caught by their children, so you're not just shaping your children's lives, but those of your grandchildren as well!

2. **Values are Taught**. It's not enough simply to hope your children will catch your values because they see them. If they don't understand them, they can't live by them and may still reject them. For most of their early lives, your kids trust your judgment completely and want to know what you think about everything. So make sure you tell them what your values are while you still have the chance. Work hard to find opportunities when you can deliberately pass on your advice, wisdom, views, opinions and beliefs to them. It would be tragic if, when they were grown-up, your children had no idea what you felt about life's important issues.

So make sure they know *why* you hold the values you do. Sit down with them for a 'quiet chat' over breakfast, or dinner in a restaurant (it needn't be expensive). Take them to the cinema, and talk about the issues the film raises. Or start a conversation while you're both doing something together. Whatever you do, don't put it off. Start today. Or the next time you turn around, they'll be grown up and it'll be too late.

'The most important thing a father can do for his children is to love their mother.'

Theodore Hesberg

Parents are the heart of the family

Secure families produce secure children. Families come in all shapes and sizes, and many of them, for one reason or another, have only one parent. However, if you have a partner, the quality of your relationship with them will have a huge impact on your children. Your relationship is at the heart of your family. So if it's a continuous war zone, this will have a detrimental effect on your kids.

In the film *Back To The Future*, Marty's parents are classic no-hopers. His dad is a pathetic creature who 'never stood up to anyone in his life'. His mum is growing old and fat and bored. And neither of them is interested in their kids or each other. As a result, Marty's brother has a dead-end job and his sister can't get a boyfriend. Only Marty has managed to break the mould. But when he accidentally gets sent back in time to 1955, he inspires his then seventeen-year-old father to stand up for himself. This changes everything. When Marty gets back home to 1985, his dad is a success, his mum is youthful and energetic, and they're both deeply in love with each other. And the effect of this? His brother is a corporate businessman, and his sister has so many boys after her that no one can keep track of them all. The self-confidence, love and relationship that Marty's parents have shapes their whole family's future.

If you have a partner, the way you are together will have just as profound an effect on your children. If you and your partner are constantly rowing, for example, it's almost bound to have an effect on your son or daughter's performance at school. It'll be virtually impossible for them to keep their minds on their lessons or homework if they're worried about things falling apart at home. What's more, they're likely to feel that they're to blame for everything. Anxiety and guilt don't motivate kids to do well at school. What they need to know is that, however tough the big world is, home is fun and secure.

When children see their parents fall out of love with each other, it's only natural for them to begin to wonder if they still love *them*. After all, if you can stop loving each other, why shouldn't you stop loving them? Of course, most parents who go through a divorce or break-up couldn't stop loving their children if they tried. But this isn't at all obvious to the children involved.

So it's vitally important that through all the loo-cleaning, kid-ferrying, clothes-washing, key-losing, meal-cooking, sink-unblocking, supermarket-shopping, cat-feeding, bill-paying, vomit-clearing, mundane tasks of everyday life, you work hard to keep the romance alive. And when it's not there, you continue working hard at loving each other through all the arguments and hard times. And don't be afraid to kiss or cuddle one another in front of the children. Knowing that you love each other helps reassure them that you love them too.

But what if things have reached the point where you and your partner are thinking seriously about separation or divorce? Is it better to stay together for the sake of the kids or not? For most of the last thirty years, the experts told us that staying together was always counter-productive. The children would know it was an empty sham. In an ideal world, of course, they'd *want* you to stay together. What child, hand on heart, *wouldn't* prefer that their mum and dad love each other? But, the argument went, children were far more robust than they were given credit for. They were mature enough to accept the fact that you couldn't stay together. What really mattered most to them was that Mum and Dad were 'both happy and free to be themselves' instead of feeling trapped.

But recent research has turned this view on its head. The days of pretending that kids don't mind whether their parents decide to split up or not are over. The fact is that all children function better in a secure and settled environment. Their schoolwork is better, their behaviour is better and they're less likely to leave home or dabble in under-age sex (often simply a misguided cry for attention and love). Except in cases of ongoing domestic violence, children are happier when their loyalties aren't being divided. They're more secure when they're not being ferried between different homes. So the view now is: if at all possible, *do* stay together for the sake of the children. They didn't ask to be born, so you owe it to them to put them first. It's nothing more than common sense, really.

If you are struggling in your relationship, it's often a good idea to get help from a professional counselling organisation like Relate. They'll be able to help you think through your problems, either on your own or, most beneficially, with your partner. Whatever you do, don't simply give up or try to sweep things under the carpet in the hope they'll just disappear. Take action and deal with them *now*! It's too important not to.

Sometimes, of course, staying together just isn't an option. Your marriage or relationship won't work. You've asked for help and done everything you know, but it makes no difference. Sometimes you don't have a choice. Your partner has walked out on you and you're on your own. And on top of all your other worries, you're very concerned about how the children are coping.

If you separate, decide to get divorced or find yourself abandoned, what can you do to help your children adjust better to their new situation?

- Never blame them for the break-up of your relationship. It's not *their* fault if *you* can't get on with your former partner. This may be obvious to you, but it's far from obvious to them. Most kids feel responsible when their parents bust-up. You must do all you can to allay their fears, which will turn into a deep sense of guilt without your reassurance. Don't wait for it to become an issue. Do all you can to get the message across. Assure them it's not their fault. Explain to them why they shouldn't feel guilty.
- Agree with your ex-partner beforehand what you're going to say to your kids. Then sit down and talk to them *together*. Explain, as simply as you can, what's going on. And if talking to them together isn't possible, at least try to agree on your story. Giving them two different versions will only leave them wondering whether they can believe either of you, and will probably lead to them inventing their own version of events.
- Tell them the truth, not half-truths. Gaps in their knowledge will quickly be filled by their imagination . . . or playground rumours.
- Divorce or separation is like bereavement. So whatever you say, expect your children to go through periods of shock, denial, resentment, anger, confusion and grief before slowly coming to terms with the situation.
- Tell them about all the practical problems, and answer all their questions as honestly as you can. They'll want to know where they are going to live and how much they'll see each of you. They'll feel very insecure and worried about big changes such as leaving their friends, school, etc.

Above all, don't use your kids as pawns in your own little power game. You're divorcing each other, not them, so don't use them as weapons or try to get at your ex-partner through them. They need the love and support of *both* of you, so never moan about each other in their presence. Whatever you may think of your ex-partner and their behaviour, don't run them down in front of your kids. Children automatically love and respect both parents. If they hear you badmouthing your ex-partner, it won't help their respect for you either.

> **'Children have never been very good at listening to their elders, but they have never failed to imitate them.'**
>
> James Baldwin

Single parents

When two parents are involved in raising a child, there's great comfort in the fact that you're not the only one on show. But for a single parent, things are different. Unless you've got a close friend or family member who can act like a kind of 'adopted' parent, the responsibility falls entirely on your shoulders. You're on show twenty-four hours a day, and there's usually no one to talk through the issues with. In effect, you're permanently ON DUTY, and that's a very demanding job. Even when you're sick, depressed or upset, you still have to run the home, maintain discipline and show your kids that you love them. And in the midst of the chores and responsibility, it can seem almost impossible to find quality time for your kids – even to talk meaningfully to them, let alone to have fun together.

To make matters even tougher, there's often still an unkind and unhelpful stigma attached to being a single parent. Some people frown on you because they seem to think for some reason that just being a single parent is a crime in itself. The truth is, of course, that people become single parents for all sorts of different reasons, that few would choose that pathway in an ideal world, and that the vast majority do a fantastic job without the kind of support and backup that two-parent families enjoy. In fact, many single parents are so aware of the potential weaknesses for their kids in their situation that they give 150 per cent of themselves, and end up doing a far better job than many families where both parents are present.

If you are a lone parent, be very careful about who else you allow to step into a position where they become a kind of 'adopted' parent and a role model for your child. Because whoever you choose, they'll begin to impose their values on your children, whether they mean to or not. So even if you feel under great pressure, make your choices very carefully.

> **'When I was a boy of fourteen, my father was so ignorant I could hardly stand to have the old man around. But when I got to be twenty-one, I was astonished at how much he had learnt in seven years.'**
>
> Mark Twain

YOU are the foundation of your child's life

Every parent is charged with the huge responsibility and the wonderful privilege and joy of being a role model and so shaping a life, perhaps even moulding someone who will one day become a parent themselves. Beyond doubt, the way we parent our children is the single most crucial factor in determining who they become. Always remember that one day, they'll look in the mirror and realise exactly how much like you they've turned out.

All parents are role models. The only question is, what kind of role models are we? How good a job are we doing?

Remember

- Parents lay the foundations of their children's lives.
- Your kids are being influenced by someone or something all day every day.
- 'Do as I say, not as I do' doesn't work. You're a role model to your children.
- All children slowly become more and more like their parents.
- Your child's values are 'taught', but they're also 'caught'.
- If possible, stay together 'for the sake of the children'.
- Single parents should choose very carefully where they get help from.

Key principles

Be the kind of person you want your child to become.

How to achieve it

- Double the amount of time you spend in meaningful conversation with your child this week – and next!
- Take the time to watch a TV soap with your kids and talk to them about the issues it raises.
- Remember that actions speak louder than words. Think about what messages your kids have caught from you this week.
- Deliberately find an opportunity to pass on one of your values to your children.

Be Clear

Establish your family rules and stick to them

'**Routine is the source of all happiness.**'

Barbara Toner

House rules are like a playpen: they give freedom within safe limits

In the film *Who Framed Roger Rabbit?*, Roger gets left in charge of baby Herman while Herman's mum is out. Safe in his playpen, Herman seems a babysitter's dream ... even for a cartoon rabbit. But then everything goes wrong. Because of Roger's stupidity, Herman escapes from his cage and crawls to the kitchen in search of the cookie jar. What follows is every mother's nightmare. Young Herman only narrowly avoids being skewered in the cutlery drawer, burned alive on the cooker, drowned in the sink, cut to pieces by kitchen knives, and splatted all over the floor when he falls off the fridge.

While baby Herman was safe in his playpen, he had freedom, but he had it within secure and sensible limits. He could choose what to do and what to play with, and was safe from harm. But once outside, life suddenly became extremely dangerous, because he lacked the wisdom and experience needed to cope without restraints.

Just as little Herman needed to be kept within the confines of his playpen for his own safety, so all children need the protection that a clear set of rules and limits offers them. Family rules act like a perimeter fence, marking the safe limits beyond which a child mustn't go, but within which they can enjoy freedom. Everything inside the boundary is safe, but everything beyond it is strictly 'out of bounds'. And this perimeter fence is set up and kept in place by their parent's authority.

Family rules, like a nation's laws, are there to give freedom within safe limits. It's no good simply telling kids to 'act your age' when they get things wrong and behave badly. Most of the time they behave as they do precisely *because* they're acting their age! That's just the point. And that's why they need rules: to protect them until they're old enough to make sensible decisions for themselves. The boundaries that family rules provide aren't just a good way of managing chaos. They're a vital part of a parent's responsibility to protect their kids from harm, and to teach them right from wrong.

Your kids, like everyone else's, will inevitably push against the boundaries you set them, to see how far they can be stretched, and even whether they can be kicked down and trampled underfoot altogether! But at the same time, they actually rely on them being there to protect them. So the boundaries you set, just like the walls of a playpen, must provide your children both with *freedom* and with *safe limits*, because they'll need *both* if they are to grow up to become constructive and responsible members of society.

There are two traps that every parent has to avoid when making family rules:

- **Being too permissive**. Allowing a child to do whatever they like whenever they like is *not* the hallmark of a loving parent. In fact, it's the exact opposite. Without well-defined boundaries of behaviour, a child will grow confused and insecure. How can they be sure what's right and what's wrong? But in fact, no home has *no* rules or boundaries. It's just that, in a home where they're not clearly set out, understood and consistently maintained, the rules that *do* get applied are usually arbitrary – totally dependent on a parent's mood. They're unpredictable, and only enforced when a parent reaches the end of their tether. The result is that a child never knows where they stand or what's expected. What's more, by not giving clear guidelines, parents only store up trouble for their children later on: having never learnt how to behave acceptably, they'll eventually come up against someone – at school, work or elsewhere – who will step in to 'teach them a lesson they'll never forget'.

- **Being too authoritarian**. In this kind of home, rigid boundaries are set in place with no discussion or understanding, and new rules are often imposed without warning or explanation. The parent's motto is, 'Jump when I say jump', and the kids don't so much live within safe boundaries as within a strait-jacket. This kind of regime leaves no room for mistakes, choices or growth. But when you don't give your kids enough freedom, they'll eventually take it from you anyway. One day they'll *do* what they want, *go* where they want, *wear* what they want, *say* what they want, and *see* who they want anyway. The big problem is that they won't have had enough experience of freedom to know how to handle it wisely.

So it's up to every sensible parent to steer a middle road, creating a flexible framework of rules, discipline and freedom that'll prepare their child to be able to make wise decisions in the future. And the goal is slowly to enlarge their 'playpen', because as they grow and develop, they'll need and will be able to handle greater and greater levels of freedom and choice, which previous, tighter limits will have taught them to handle wisely. Strict rules gradually give way to trust. All this means that by the time they're able to break down the perimeter fences altogether, they won't want to. By then, they'll appreciate and enjoy living in a way that both respects and protects others as well as themselves.

> **'A caged bird is well fed and safe from next door's cat. But a bird is born to fly, not sit on a perch for life.'**
>
> Anonymous

Plan ahead: develop rules BEFORE you need them

Many parents spend their whole time involved in 'crisis management'. No sooner has one domestic catastrophe been dealt with than another explodes. It's impossible, of course, to predict every disciplinary problem that will hit your home, and you are bound to have your fair share of crises, just like every other family. But the truth is that some families have far *more* than their fair share of crises, simply because they don't think and plan ahead. A little advance planning can save you a great deal of hassle.

So the key is to think about and develop your family rules *before* you need them. Why? Because:

- Sooner or later you *will* need them. Don't fool yourself into thinking you won't. Instead, take the time to think through the issues and talk to other parents you respect, and who've been there before you, about their approach. If you don't plan ahead, establishing your family rules firmly in your own mind and telling your kids about them and the issues that surround them, you'll probably end up making hot-headed decisions on the spur of the moment that you'll later regret.

- You can't expect your children to do what you say unless you've told them in advance what that is. They're not mindreaders, and they're not likely to be able to guess. So make sure they know exactly where they stand by stating clearly and ahead of time what the rules are.

- Making clear and well-thought-out rules before you actually need them will help your child to understand why they exist in the first place. In other words, a rule is never enough on its own. 'Do as I say and don't argue' is never the best policy. It's always better to back up any rules you impose with clear information and open discussion on why they need to be there. The more understanding a child has as to why family rules exist, the more responsible their behaviour will tend to be (though you do need to remember they're still kids!), and the fewer rules you'll actually need.

RECKON WE SHOULD MAKE SOME FAMILY RULES!

WELL THEY'RE MUCH TOO IMPORTANT TO RULE OUT...

Lots of parents worry about how they're going to cope with having a 'dreaded teenager'. The truth is that though a teenager will always be a challenge, they can also be a whole lot of fun. The secret is this: the time to diffuse the 'teenage time-bomb' is ten years before it's due to go off. If your three-year-old knows they can get whatever they want by throwing a tantrum, don't blame them if they're still doing the same thing at thirteen. To avoid a crisis at thirteen, fourteen or fifteen, you need to start work on your child's problems when they're still only three, four or five years old.

> **'Children are a great comfort in your old age –
> and they help you reach it faster too.'**
>
> Lionel Kaufman

Choose your battles carefully

The closeness of family life has a way of catching you off guard, getting under your skin and making you lose your cool over the wrong things. So a minor incident gets turned into a full-scale drama. You know how it is: your toddler wants to wear his favourite red T-shirt rather than the clean blue one you put out for him, or your daughter wants to get her nose pierced. Your reaction is to go ballistic and turn the issue into World War III. It's just so easy to get worked up and blow a fuse over things that don't really matter.

Many of the things we get most worked up about just aren't worth fighting over. The world isn't going to end because your daughter is fifteen minutes late home from a date, or because her skirt is only ten inches from the waist to the hem. It won't even end if she comes home one day with a rose tattooed on her shoulder. These things seem very serious at the time, but they're not worth flying off the deep end over. Many parents become so concerned with winning the battle that they lose the war. They lose their sense of proportion, and eventually their relationship with their children, over unimportant issues. Trust is destroyed over nothing. As a result, their kids reject their help, support and guidance when it really matters.

So try to keep things in perspective. Don't allow arguments and disagreements over minor issues to get in the way of your relationship with your children. Only draw a line in the sand when you're sure you really want it to be there. And as you draw up your family rules, remember that:

- Rules are there to teach your kids freedom within safe limits. If you don't allow them to make their own decisions – and mistakes – within those limits, they will never learn to handle freedom properly. Always stop and ask yourself, 'Does it really matter?' Rules are there only for protection, so try to let them choose for themselves unless their safety is threatened. If your six-year-old boy wants to wear his red T-shirt instead of the blue one, let him. But if he wants to play Saw-The-Lady-In-Half with his sister and a *real* saw, get tough!
- Going to war over little things is like crying wolf too often. If you make a big deal over something that doesn't really matter, how are your kids supposed to know when things *do* matter? By choosing your battles more carefully, you save your heavy artillery for things that are really important, and your children will know that it matters and you do mean business.
- Once a battle starts, the stakes are very high. If you say 'No' over something important, but then back down and let your kids walk all over you, they'll try the same thing again and again in the future. So it's vital that you choose your battles carefully, only going to war over things that really matter, and then make it clear you're *not* bluffing. Otherwise you'll find yourself having to win a war that wasn't even worth fighting to begin with.
- Too much conflict makes everyone battle-weary. There are

bound to be times when you argue with your kids. After all, you want the best for them. You want them to make their own decisions, but you want these to be good ones. Some parent/child conflict is inevitable in any family, but be careful because constant warfare is sure to ruin your relationship.

> **'Dad, dad, when you come up to give us a bit of real trouble, can you bring us up a drink of water as well?'**
>
> Michael Rosen, *These Two Children*

Have fewer rules rather than lots of them

Having just a few rules is better than having lots of them. Even God only gave the human race ten Commandments, not 250! So don't fall into the trap of making too many. The more rules you make, the more you have to remember . . . and enforce. Your rules should be reasonable and necessary. But above all, learn a lesson from the mistakes governments make: don't create laws you can't enforce. Instead, decide what really matters, and only make rules about these things. Keep them to a minimum.

For instance, there are four main rules in our house which cover virtually everything else. We've phrased these rules positively, not negatively:

1. Always tell the truth.
2. Always show other people courtesy, care and respect.
3. Always work together as a family and talk about problems.
4. Always remember that trust needs to be earned.

These are the basis for other, more specific rules that change as time passes, and aren't rigid or etched in stone, but are more or less understood anyway: tidy your bedroom, don't hog the computer, go to bed at the right time, do your homework when you first get it, clean out the rabbit hutch on Saturday morning, etc.

Don't have a huge number of rules, but make sure that those you have are clearly understood by everyone. And it's better to phrase them as positive goals than as a list of 'thou shalt nots'. From the Garden of Eden to Al Capone, prohibitions haven't worked all that well. It's almost as though there's something about a firm command *not* to do something that makes us immediately want to go out and have a go at it! So whenever you can, develop rules that stress something positive.

You'd be surprised how well this can work. When one of my sons finally found the courage to tell me that he'd made a small hole in the dining room window by catapulting a stone through it earlier that day, he was shaking from head to foot. He was probably convinced that the world – or at least *his* world – was about to end. He knows that throwing stones in the garden isn't allowed, let alone propelling them by catapult. But it showed great strength of character for him to tell me the truth when he didn't have to, so I wasn't furious that he'd broken a small rule. He knew he'd made a bad mistake already. Instead, without letting him feel that his 'crime' didn't matter, I made sure he knew how proud of him I was for owning up, and keeping our first family rule: always tell the truth. That day, we reinforced three lessons:

1. Truth is more important than windows.
2. It always pays to tell the truth, however hard it might seem at the time.
3. Think about the possible consquences of an action before you take it.

My only alternative response (which I admit was a rather tempting one) – flying off the handle and shouting threats at him in a deafeningly loud voice – might have made me feel better in the short term, but in the long term would simply have taught him to cover his tracks better and learn how to lie more effectively!

If your kids know that you value their honesty, and love them no matter what, they will feel able to admit when they've done something wrong. And they'll slowly feel able to come and talk to you about other things as well. But when family rules are just a long list of *don'ts*, parents seem more like judges than friends.

Of course, *don'ts* are always necessary, but they should never overshadow the *do*s. The more positive you make your family rules, the more effective they'll be. And the more your kids will feel able to talk to you about what's on their mind. In fact, this is one of the best ways you can give your children freedom within safe limits, because by talking things through with them, you can begin to help them learn how to make safe and sensible choices. And at the same time, you also avoid the need for so many negative rules as they get older.

> **'Live so that, when your children think of fairness and integrity, they think of you.'**
>
> Anonymous

Make sure your rules are reasonable

Make sure that your house rules, and the consequences of breaking them, are both reasonable. For instance, if your son decides to do a Jimi Hendrix impression on his guitar at 2 a.m. – with the amplifier blasting out three giga-watts of raw power and deafening everyone within a three-mile radius – it's better to insist on a maximum volume and strict practice times in future than to ban the amp altogether.

Too authoritarian a household, where rules seem to be enforced with no logical basis, will stifle your children in just the same way that too permissive a household will spoil them.

Remember, you're a family, not a court of law. Your rules are meant to be there to protect your children and others from harm, enhancing their lives and increasing their fun. If their only purpose appears to be to restrict their freedom, your kids will begin to disobey them as soon as they're clever enough or bold enough to do so.

RULE NUMBER ONE...

UNDER NO CIRCUMSTANCES HAVE NEGATIVE RULES!

The older your children get, the more involved they can – and *should* – be in shaping family rules in the first place. They can even agree the punishments for breaking them. Though your family isn't a democracy – you're the boss – by acting as if it *were* a lot of the time, you can help train your children to take responsibility for their own lives. If they feel they 'own' the rules, they'll be less likely to break them and more inclined to accept the penalties when they do.

But remember, they'll find it difficult to agree to rules that don't make any sense to them. And even if they do agree, they'll resent them, and you for making them. So you need to think about your rules carefully, and how to explain them so that they make sense to your children. The more your rules make sense to your kids, the more likely they are to be accepted.

But watch out: the rules you make are likely to include

checks on *your* behaviour as well! Like it or not, you undermine your own rules whenever you violate them or unreasonably claim they don't apply to you. It confuses kids when adults seem to play by a whole different set of rules. If you make a rule that doesn't apply to you, you'll need to explain clearly and convincingly *why* you're exempt. The more fair and reasonable your total package of rules is, the easier this task will be.

There's a big difference, of course, between challenging a rule because you think it's unjust, and simply breaking it. When your children are young, they'll inevitably bend a rule just to see how firm it is. This is a direct challenge to your authority, and you'll end up losing that authority if you don't enforce the rule. For instance, when you tidy up your three-year-old son's toys because it's time for bed, and he just tips them out over the floor again, he's testing you. What do you do? Do you say something like, 'Naughty boy,' and pick them all up again, just for him to repeat the process? Or do you lose your temper and make all sorts of threats that you don't mean and which, for all the noise, still don't teach him not to throw toys all over the floor? Screams and empty threats won't win you the day. You'll only win your child's respect if you're both firm and loving. So keep calm and exert your authority by putting your hands over his and gently making him put the toys back with you, before taking him up to bed. As much as anything, he's asking, 'Who's in charge?' And he needs a clear answer in order to feel secure.

But as they get older and start to work things out for themselves, your kids are far more likely to break a rule because it doesn't make sense to them. This is a totally different matter. If they're right, and the rule is unreasonable, you'll only lose authority and respect by enforcing it. But if they're wrong, you could still lose authority and respect if you don't explain the reasons why the rule exists in a clear, calm and logical way.

In fact, getting the balance right, and slowly allowing your kids to replace *your* rules with *their* judgment as they get older, is one of the most difficult challenges any parent faces. Some rules obviously come with built-in 'sell-by' dates. 'Don't cross the road on your own,' for instance, or, 'Don't lock the bathroom door when you're in there alone' won't be appropriate forever. But unfortunately there's no chart available setting out the precise schedule for the move from a strict set of rules to greater freedom and trust. And even if there were, it would be useless. Each child is unique: they handle responsibility in their own way and in their own time, which means that once again it's the time you invest in getting to know your child – its quantity and quality – that will be your best guide.

> **'The thing that impresses me most about America is the way parents obey their children.'**
> Edward VIII, Duke of Windsor

If a rule is worth having, it's worth enforcing

Every bad rule you make – and every good rule you fail to enforce – eats away at your authority. That's why it's vital to think carefully about your rules *before* you make them. Then you'll know that they really do matter, and why. If you're not going to enforce a rule, it's better not to make it in the first place. Empty threats and endless nagging are useless because your child knows there's no substance behind them. If you tell them firmly not to do something, and they do it anyway, and you don't punish them, what have they learnt? Answer: That they can do whatever they like in life, without having to face the consequences.

Jenny is watching TV in the lounge. Her son, Tim, plays with his Lego on the floor by her feet. 'Time for bed . . . now,' she says sternly. But interestingly, neither of them moves a muscle for a good ten minutes. Then she repeats her command, louder and more sternly. Tim begins to sense that the dreaded moment is creeping up on him, so he says, 'OK . . . in a minute.' But again, neither of them moves. At the start of the next ad break, Jenny lays down the law: 'I really mean it, get up those stairs NOW!' Tim knows it's time to make some kind of token gesture, and slowly begins to pack up his Lego. But he's been here before, and he knows that whatever she says, she won't do anything until the end of the programme.

What does Tim learn from all this? His mum has shown him very effectively how he can manipulate a situation in order to get his own way.

- Her first mistake was starting with an unreasonable command. If instead she'd announced that bedtime was in fifteen minutes, the element of surprise would have gone. He'd have had time to get used to the idea. And just as importantly, she'd have shown Tim that she respected what he was doing and didn't just want to spoil his fun.
- The fatal error was *not moving* when she told him to go upstairs. This sent out conflicting signals. Her words told him to go, but her body language said that it wouldn't really matter if he didn't. According to experts, only about 10 per cent of our communication is verbal. The actual words we use have less impact than how we say them and what we do. Jenny wanted to see the end of the TV show more than she wanted Tim to go to bed, and this came out in her voice, her body language and her actions – or lack of them! If she'd got up to go with him, he'd have known that she meant what she said. Instead, she just taught Tim to persevere until he got what he wanted. And she undermined her own authority into the bargain.

By the same token, if a rule clearly isn't having the desired effect then it's better to scrap it than to carry on enforcing it. Enforcing a rule that, for all its good intentions, just doesn't work tells your children that you're more interested in their obedience than their welfare, and this will gradually undermine all your authority.

'Every generation rebels against its fathers and makes friends with its grandfathers.'

Lewis Mumford

Agree your rules with your partner well in advance

Children can be very good at playing one parent off against another. How many times have your kids asked you for permission to do something when, unknown to you, your partner has already said they can't? And when you say 'Yes', you get it in the neck from your partner, who feels that their authority has been pulled from under their feet like a rug. And how often, in trying to avoid this situation, have you asked, 'Well, what did Mummy/Daddy say?', so giving an open invitation for your child to 'bend' the truth a little? It's very rare for a son or daughter to turn around and admit, 'Well, they actually said no, but I was hoping you'd give me a better answer, and that's why I asked.'

Instead of asking your child what your partner thinks, go and ask them yourself. Better still, whenever you can, stay ahead of the game by discussing things with your partner and agreeing rules together well in advance – united you stand, divided you fall!

But however united you are, there are simply loads of occasions when you find yourself taken by surprise. Your child asks for permission to do something that requires an instant, 'on the spot' judgment, and your partner is nowhere to be seen. 'Can I have one of those chocolate bars?' 'Can I have a Coke with my lunch?' 'Can I go out to the cinema tonight? I need to know now, because Heather's waiting on the phone and she needs to book the tickets.' In these cases, you'll need to decide one way or the other, and later explain your decision to your partner if they have strong views to the contrary. (The only alternative is to have literally *millions* of rules, covering every possible eventuality!) You're bound to make the odd slip-up, and you'll have to live through the resulting tension. It's only natural, and everybody does it. But as long as you're getting it right together more often than not, you'll be OK.

If you're a single parent, and you have any kind of help from a parent, friend, neighbour, childminder or babysitter, then you face just the same problem. It's up to you to make sure that your family rules are properly understood and enforced by everyone who looks after your kids. Otherwise you may find that all your careful discipline is being undone every time their grandma or granddad comes to babysit, for example. You're responsible for what goes on in your house, so brief your helpers.

And if you're divorced or separated from the father or mother of your child or children, and they spend time in both homes, you still need to agree on what kind of rules they should live by. Dads who see their kids only on weekends and holidays, for instance, can easily fall into the trap of spoiling them. Sometimes this is a kind of emotional bribe: a way of trying to 'buy' their affection by giving them presents or allowing them to do things their mum never lets them do. Sometimes it's even a deliberate attempt to get back at their former partner. But it's usually just a case of not thinking through the consequences properly. Children need stability and routine. Things must be predictable. They don't yet have the mental or emotional resources to cope with constant or dramatic changes. In fact, part of the reason for having family rules in the first place is to give them this stability. So if the rules at Mum's house are totally different from the rules at Dad's, rather than ending up with the best of both worlds, they're more likely to end up with neither.

That means that if your children live with your ex-partner, not with you, you may need to be a little more flexible when you both sit down to agree the rules, which you then must stick to. If you don't, it's your children rather than your ex-partner who will suffer in the end.

Remember

- Family rules give kids freedom within safe limits.
- It's important, whenever you can, to have rules in place before you need them.
- A few rules are better than many, but make sure they're enforceable.
- Choose your battles carefully: don't go to war over things that don't matter.
- Rules should be agreed to, and stuck to, by everyone (including you).
- There's no point in making a rule if you're not going to enforce it properly.
- Strict rules should gradually give way to greater degrees of trust.
- Be united: agree rules with your partner, if you have one.

Key principles

Work out four positive family rules you'd want your home to run by.

How to achieve it

- Think about the qualities you want your children to develop, and make your rules around them.
- Make your rules positive, not negative.
- Make sure your rules are clear and practical.
- Either enforce a rule or remove it. Don't have it and ignore it.

Be Prepared

Things can, and always will, go wrong

> 'Heredity is what a man believes in until his son begins to behave like a delinquent.'
>
> *Presbyterian Life*

Things will always go wrong

We've all seen it on TV, and it makes us sick. Breakfast scenes filled with happy, smiling faces and families, laughing, joking and talking together in wonderfully decorated, brightly furnished, spacious homes. The sun is shining, the birds are singing, the freshly squeezed orange juice is flowing, and everyone is looking forward to another glorious day.

Our house is different. Everyone is late and everything is rushed. I can't find my shoes, one of the kids can't find their homework, and the milk gets spilled over the kitchen table. A bitter argument breaks out over who's going to have the free plastic dinosaur in the cornflakes packet, and who had it last time. Someone steps on the cat. Cornelia and I can't quite agree on who last had the car keys. I'm convinced it was her, and point out that she's always losing things and it's about time she got a grip of herself . . . until, that is, I find them in my coat pocket and accuse one of the kids of putting them there.

However much you dream of, and even plan for, it all to go right, things can and always will go wrong . . . usually at the worst possible moment! The reason for this is simple: you're not a perfect parent, your kids aren't perfect children, and your family is therefore not one of those perfect Hollywood families.

THE ONLY THING I KNOW I'M RIGHT ABOUT IS THAT THINGS WILL ALWAYS GO WRONG...

So what do you do when it all goes horribly, terribly and drastically wrong? What happens when it's not a 'tool kit' of disciplinary techniques you need, but rather a full-blown repair kit? What happens when you've read everything this book has to say about love, discipline, praise and consistency, and thought, 'Great, but it's too late for me! I'm a failure!' It's all a bit like trying to close the stable door after the horse has bolted and is three miles down the road. You've lost your temper, again. You've been totally inconsistent. Your kids don't think you love them, and relationships are 'icy', to put it mildly. Where do you go from here? How do you make peace? How do you start again?

The first thing to do is understand that you *can* make amends, however bad things seem to be at the moment. Your relationship with your children has an incredible natural ability to heal itself, if you let it. Why? The reason is very simple. Your kids *want* to forgive you. They *need* to love you. They desperately *want* to trust you, and enjoy a good relationship with you. And they need *your* love and respect, more than you can ever possibly imagine, in order to live full and healthy lives.

All this gives you a massive advantage as you work hard to put things right with them. So the task ahead isn't as impossible as it might at first seem, because making up and healing the hurts is something they actively want to do.

It'll take time, perhaps a long time. But the damage can be healed. A 'flashpoint' incident, where anger has flared up quickly over something specific, is obviously a lot easier to deal with and heal than long-term relationship failure, where bitterness and resentment have slowly built up over many years. But strangely, exactly the same 'medicine' is used to treat both problems – all that's different is the recovery time.

> **'Living together is the most difficult thing there is because it is all about constant tolerance and forgiveness.'**
>
> Arthur Miller

Love means always having to say you're sorry

The only line anyone ever remembers from the film *Love Story* is: 'Love means never having to say you're sorry.' But the truth is, love means *constantly* having to say you're sorry. No one's perfect, and all parents make loads of mistakes, just like you. But the good news is that you can turn a minus into a plus. We can all make positive use of even our foul-ups.

How? We all want our children to be honest and brave enough to admit when they've made mistakes. If they've done something to hurt us or someone else, we want them to be big enough to own up, apologise and ask for forgiveness. But how can they possibly learn to do this if *we* never admit to *our* mistakes or apologise ourselves?

Let's face it: we send our children mixed messages all the time. Some of these messages are good, and some are bad. It'd be great to think that we were always in total control of the kind of signals we give out, but a lot of the time this just isn't the case. Even when we manage to use all the right words, we can still upset people because of *how* we say them. For instance, if we've had a bad day, it'll usually show in the tone of our voice.

And it's not just how *we* say things. It's how we react to the things others say to us. We're inconsistent. If we're in a bad mood, we snap at people not because of anything they've said, but just because they're unfortunate enough to be in the wrong place at the wrong time and come face to face with us. Sometimes an exhausted or exasperated parent will even trigger a bitter, and perhaps long-lasting, rift by over-reacting to their kids with such classic lines as, 'If you do that once more, you'll never show your face in this house again!', and then not having the courage to back down immediately afterwards. The truth is that we all blow it from time to time because we're only human.

In business, my friend Andrew was a real diplomat. Though he had strong views and opinions, his job – which involved dealing with people all over the world, from very different cultures – constantly required him to make the effort to be both tactful and charming. But when he got home, it was a different story. He was a good dad, and loved his kids very much. But he never showed them the same tact and courtesy he had to show others. He was never as patient, and far more stubborn. He rarely made the same effort at home as he did at work. After all, if he couldn't relax and be himself with his family, who *could* he relax and be himself with? They'd understand.

As the saying goes, 'people always save their worst behaviour for home'. Even the best parents in the world have weak spots and get things wrong. In fact, we often treat our family worse than we treat strangers. We have to spend so long being 'nice' to people outside the home that by the end of the day we're exhausted. Our patience has run out. So when our kids do something to annoy us, we lash out, unloading our anger and frustration on them. We just don't feel we've got the energy to be courteous or tolerant any more.

But whatever our excuse, whenever we take our family for granted, we're paving the way for eventual tension and division. By saving our worst behaviour for home, we're giving our kids the impression that they're not important enough to us to get better treatment. Of course, none of us believe this, but it's the message we send out anyway. Sadly, our children can't see our attitudes or feelings – all they can see is our behaviour. So it's something for which we need to say sorry.

> **'There are times when parenthood seems nothing but feeding the mouth that bites you.'**
>
> Peter de Vries

Apologising isn't a sign of weakness. It's a sign of strength

Some parents are worried that apologising to their kids will be seen as a sign of weakness. They're concerned that any chink in their armour will be exploited. If they come across as 'weak', their child will lose respect both for them and the rules they're trying to enforce. Or they're worried that by apologising for what *they've* said and done, they'll come across as accepting – or, worse still, even condoning – the bad things their kids have said and done. But, in fact, it's parents who can never admit when they themselves are in the wrong who eventually lose their children's respect.

Apologising when you've hurt someone isn't a sign of weakness. It's actually a sign of strength. Rather than undermining your authority, it sets a good example. It encourages your kids to apologise themselves when they've done something wrong. And it also builds trust and softens the atmosphere.

Learning to apologise is very hard, especially when you're feeling insecure and lacking in self-confidence . . . which, of course, is *exactly* how a child feels when they're at the receiving end of your anger or insensitivity. It's only if they feel secure and unthreatened that they will begin to find the strength to admit their mistakes and ask forgiveness. So even if you think your child is completely in the wrong, by apologising for any harsh words or personal attacks you made when *you* reacted, you're making it easier for *them* to learn to apologise both to you and to others.

But there's another, more common reason why parents don't apologise to their kids, and it's a lot simpler. In fact, it's the same reason why they don't praise them enough: they're just not in the habit. It's difficult to say sorry. Our mistakes don't exactly show us in the best light, so we want to ignore or forget them, not focus on them. By apologising, we're having to face up to the fact that we're capable of hurting people, either from cruelty or carelessness. And we're also admitting that we care about the people we've hurt, enough to feel bad and want to put things right. The problem is that this kind of emotional honesty, especially when we're not used to it, can be very embarrassing, which is why it's a habit that most of us just don't have.

Nevertheless, learning how to apologise and ask for forgiveness when you've treated your child unfairly is a habit that is well worth working on, because:

- An apology can melt resentment and create respect, which helps pave the way for forgiveness and reconciliation on both sides.
- An apology sets an example, helping your child build the confidence to admit when *they've* done wrong or hurt someone.
- An apology shows your child that they can admit their errors without losing face.
- An apology shows your child that failure isn't a kind of unforgivable sin, and it's OK to make mistakes – it's something everyone does, even you.
- An apology shows respect, telling your child that they're valuable to you and you care about how they think and feel.

> **'It's a wonderful feeling when your father becomes not a god but a man to you – when he comes down from the mountain and you see he's this man with weaknesses. And you love him as this whole being, not as a figurehead.'**
>
> Robin Williams

You can make your mistakes work FOR you

In fact, if you're prepared to admit to your failures and weaknesses, you can even use them to bring about something positive. You can actually mould them so that they become part of the positive influence you have on your children. Though this must never become an excuse for making them, by showing your kids that they're not the only ones who make mistakes and get things wrong, you're teaching them that failure in one area or another is acceptable, even inevitable. For the first years of their lives, you're a real hero to your children. You are the most important person in their world. As far as they can see, you know everything there is to know, and there's nothing you can't do. It takes a long time for them to learn the important lesson that you're fallible, and the equally important one that being fallible is OK.

My friend Karen says that the greatest thing her father ever did for her was crash the car! It's not that her dad was a bad father. In fact, if he hadn't been such a good dad, crashing the car would never have made such an impact on her. Karen's dad was kind and loving, and on top of that he seemed to have an almost encyclopaedic knowledge of virtually everything except pop music. But all this made Karen only too aware of the huge mountain she had to climb to become like him. And then, when she was fourteen, he crashed the car. No one was hurt, but Karen was never the same again. She'd seen the accident coming, but hadn't said anything because she'd assumed that he must have seen it too. By accidentally crashing the car, her dad hadn't just shown her that it was all right to make mistakes. Without knowing it, he'd also shown her that she saw things he didn't, and that he needed her just as much as she needed him.

> **'How easily a father's tenderness is recalled and how quickly a son's offences vanish at the slightest word of repentance.'**
>
> Molière

It's YOUR move!

Almost every adult has some incident etched into their memory of when they felt that their parents treated them unfairly. Children have an acute sense of fairness and very long memories. So if you don't apologise for the times you treat them badly, it can cause great resentment later on. Though it's true that time can 'heal all wounds', in reality it's just as likely to make them worse. If problems aren't resolved, they can create a barrier that just gets higher as time goes on.

It might not seem fair, but if things have gone wrong between you and your child, it's up to you as the parent to make the first move to put them right. If you've got upset with each other and have fallen out, don't wait for them to apologise and somehow change the situation. It doesn't matter how much you think they were to blame for causing it in the first place: you're an adult and they're not. So it's *your* responsibility to offer the olive branch.

- **If it was your fault**, begin by apologising. Say something like, 'I'm not feeling myself today, and I took it out on you. I know I shouldn't have, and I'm sorry.' Or, 'It was silly of me to get so upset and shout at you. I wish I'd never done it. I'm sorry.' Whatever you do, make sure that your apology is *sincere*. Though it's all right to give reasons for your actions, don't make lame excuses or try to defend them. Most of us are pretty good at twisting apologies so far round that in the end they become attacks: 'I'm sorry. I know I shouldn't have lashed out at you, but the truth is that you were wrong to say what you did and I think you deserved it. You're so ungrateful.' This kind of 'apology' is almost guaranteed to spark off another row, and make things even worse.

MY PARENTS AREN'T AFRAID TO ADMIT THEY MAKE MISTAKES.

ANYTHING ELSE WOULD BE A BIG MISTAKE.

- **If you were *mostly* or *partly* to blame**, then bite the bullet and own up. Admit to what *you* did wrong, and don't try to justify it. Most family fights are a case of 'six of one and half a dozen of another'. And though they begin small, they quickly escalate into something close to full-scale nuclear armageddon, usually because no one wants to back down and admit they were wrong, even though they know they were. By making the first move, you'll make it much easier for your child to admit their own mistakes. They're probably feeling bad about what they said or did. So if you give the lead, they may be able to admit they were also wrong, and say sorry for their part in things. But even if they don't, you've still defused the situation and given them lots to think about and learn from.

- **If it *wasn't* your fault *at all***, you still need to make the first move. But even if you're absolutely convinced beyond a shadow of doubt that the whole thing was their fault, and there's no blame whatsoever on your side of the fence, *don't say so!* You'll only put your child on the defensive again, even if they were ready to apologise. It's a natural reaction, when someone attacks you, to attempt to defend yourself. So try to say something comforting and constructive instead: 'I guess your day was horrible. So was mine. But I really don't like arguing. Let's put this behind us.'

Of course, the first move may not always be successful. Even if you bend over backwards to be forgiving – and set a new World Record for Humility – it may not produce the kind of response you were hoping for. In fact, your love and kindness may even seem to go totally unnoticed. So don't expect too much too soon. If you've been going through a difficult patch, things won't improve overnight. You'll need to stick at it, slowly breaking down the resentment, pain or distrust that exists.

By making the first move, you're building a bridge between

you and your child. They need to get things sorted out even more than you do. But they don't have the knowledge, self-confidence or maturity to begin building bridges on their own. So it's up to you to make a start. It's your job to begin creating an atmosphere of trust rather than hostility between you. But be careful: if you start coming across the bridge you've just built with all guns blazing, don't be surprised if your child blows it up again.

What do you do when your steps towards peace have been rejected? Well, if your pride is more important to you than peace with your son or daughter, then what you say is, 'I tried,' and walk away. But if you're really serious about ending the rift between you, then you'll simply have to make the *second* move as well as the first. And if that doesn't work either, you'll have to make the *third* move. And the *fourth*. And the *fifth*. And however many more moves it takes to rebuild an atmosphere of trust. So however disappointing the initial response to your overtures of peace might be, keep your cool and keep going. Don't lose your temper and shout, or you'll find yourself back at square one.

> **'I love children, but I'm not sure I could eat a whole one!'**
>
> Anonymous

Don't allow disputes to last

It's always tragic to hear about family rows that have rumbled on for years, particularly when parents and children are no longer even on speaking terms as a result. Mums and dads refuse to have anything to do with their kids. Sons and daughters have no time for their parents. Sometimes the causes for a family division are hidden so deep in the past that no one can really remember why they started in the first place. And in other cases, the initial reasons seem to be almost trivial.

Ken didn't approve of his daughter Amy's fiancé, John. He refused even to go to their wedding, let alone give her away. This hurt Amy a lot. She needed her dad's love and approval. Not going to her wedding was as though he was denying that he even had a daughter. But Ken was also hurt. And by marrying John anyway, Amy seemed to be telling him that she didn't care what he thought.

The whole family was affected. Ken's wife and other children were placed in an impossible position. If they took sides, either Ken or Amy would never speak to them again. But if they refused to take sides, *neither* of them would forgive them. The worst thing was, Amy had no idea *why* her dad didn't approve of John. The truth is that it was all to do with an unfortunate first impression. But because they never actually sat down and talked about it, things slowly just got worse and worse. Neither of them was prepared to make the first move. Now they refuse to speak to each other altogether.

Once a rift is in place, it doesn't matter how it came about. Unless *both* sides are prepared to forgive, there will never be a reconciliation. But even if your children are now adults, you're still their parent. That means it's *still* your job to make the first move and be the first one to forgive and ask forgiveness. This is not a matter for debate: it goes with the territory.

The longer you put it off, the harder it gets. The walls of resentment get higher, and things get harder to work out, not easier. There's a great deal of common sense in an old saying from the Bible: 'Don't let the sun go down when you're still angry.' In other words, the quicker you can settle a dispute, the less damage it'll do. So don't put off making the first move. Even if an argument has been going on for a long time, do something to end it *today*! Start by deciding that, rather than trying to apportion blame, you'll just forgive.

'In every dispute between parent and child, both cannot be right, but they may be, and usually are,

**both wrong. It is this situation which gives family
life its peculiar hysterical charm.'**

Isaac Rosenfeld

There are lessons to be learnt from industry

When negotiations break down between a work force and the
management of a company, there's little to be gained if the two
sides just stand on their soap boxes and trot out their rhetoric.
This kind of approach is guaranteed to generate vast quantities of
heat, but hardly any light. Progress can only be made when both
sides are prepared to sit down and discuss the whole thing
sensibly. There are important lessons to be learnt from the world
of industrial relations, ones that apply equally to family life:

- The success of negotiations depends on both sides being
  willing to listen to each other's concerns and demands.
  It's surprising how much you can achieve just by listening
  to each other. In fact, *most* problems in the home are either
  caused or made worse by one side not listening to the
  other. Often parents are so busy with their own concerns
  that they don't pick up on their children's hurts and needs,
  and their legitimate grievances. Or else the atmosphere has
  become so hostile and the relationship has deteriorated so
  far that, rather than listening to what their child is saying,
  parents use the time their child spends talking preparing
  ways to knock holes in their argument once they pause for
  breath.
- The success of negotiations also depends on
  compromise. Sometimes, of course, compromise just isn't
  possible. A firm stand needs to be taken. But most of the
  time, all that really stands in the way of compromise is
  pride. It's the same with parenting. Many rows are caused
  by parents or children digging their heels in and not giving

way on something because it would hurt their pride. It's not a question of safety or discipline. They just don't want to give in. Once again, it's up to you to make the first move and swallow your pride. Many parents fear that compromising would seriously undermine their authority. But it's important to realise that a compromise is not a surrender, so don't confuse the two. Instead, like an apology, a compromise actually shows that you respect and understand your child's feelings and wishes. And if you don't listen to their *reasonable* complaints, they'll eventually stop respecting your authority. Compromise is two-sided, so you won't be the only one giving ground. Compromise changes a conflict (win-lose) situation into one where both sides work together to find a win-win solution. For instance, if you want to spend Saturday shopping and decorating, and your kids want to go swimming and to the park, then spend the morning in the shops and go swimming with them in the afternoon.

- In extreme cases, when both sides come to a total stalemate they may have to call in **arbitration**. This is when they let someone else help them reach an agreement – someone acceptable to both sides, with a more objective view of the situation. The arbiter is there to help both sides listen to each other without going ballistic, and to help them find a way forward. When nothing else works, you may need to rely on some form of arbitration to end a row – your partner, or another trusted family member, or a good friend, or perhaps even a professional counsellor. As always, it's up to you to suggest it, and so show willing to give ground.

> **'Children begin by loving their parents; as they grow older they judge them; sometimes they forgive them.'**
>
> Oscar Wilde, *The Picture of Dorian Gray*

Touch can be an important way of saying, 'I love you'

Arguments can upset kids even more than adults. So if your child has been upset either by you or someone else, and you're trying to get them talking, be careful not to give them the 'third degree'. Make statements rather than asking confrontational questions. 'You look sad,' for instance, is a much better conversation starter than, 'Why are you sad?' It gives them the opportunity to respond without putting them on the spot. But don't be disappointed if, in spite of your overtures, they still won't respond. They just may not be up to talking or thinking rationally if they're upset.

This is where using touch can be important. It can make a big statement. Instead of talking, just holding your son's or daughter's hand, or giving them a hug, tells them loud and clear that you love them in spite of everything. However, if they still don't respond as warmly as you'd like, respect their wishes. Don't get upset, or try to force a response from them.

- Get used to rejections, and if they reject your touch, don't force it or try harder. Give them the space they need. They may only be prepared to let you sit on the end of the bed, or next to them as they watch TV. The important thing is just to let them know you're ready and willing to talk when they are.
- If they want a hug, don't turn them away. Even if you don't feel much like touching or talking, the onus is still on *you* to do all you can to heal the wound. That's because it's *always* your job to make the first moves towards peace. It may not seem fair, but then parenting isn't really about getting a fair deal. Instead, as Bill Cosby once said, 'It's a parent's responsibility not to get tired of what they've got every right to get tired of!' It's always up to you to begin again. And though it's hard, it's worth it in the long run.

Remember

- However hard you try, things will always go wrong.
- When things do go wrong, your relationship with your kids can be healed.
- If you love someone, you constantly need to say, 'I'm sorry'.
- Apologising is a habit all parents have to get into.
- If you're willing to apologise, you can turn a minus into a plus.
- As the parent, it's always up to you to make the first move.
- Don't put off mending a rift – the longer you leave it, the harder it is.
- It's vital for you to listen to what your children have to say.
- Touch is an important way of saying, 'I love you'.

Key principles

Learn to say sorry when you're in the wrong.

How to achieve it

- Remember that admitting your mistakes is not a sign of weakness. Everyone says and does things they regret.
- Recognise that your kids want to forgive you when you've treated them badly.
- Give reasons for your mistakes, but never try to justify them.
- It's your responsibility to make the first, second, third, fourth and fifth moves.

Be Flexible

Learn to let go of your children

> 'The world is going through troubled times. Today's young people only think of themselves. They've got no respect for parents or old people. They've got no time for rules or regulations. To hear them talk, you'd think they knew everything. And what we think of as wise, they just see as foolish. As for the girls, they don't speak, act or dress with any kind of modesty or feminine grace.'
>
> Peter the Monk AD 1274

Your children will soon leave home, so start getting them ready NOW!

Mr and Mrs Jones sat in their armchairs, sipping tea. They were glued to their TV set as David Attenborough explained the nesting habits of *Erithacus Rubecula*: the red-breasted robin. A hidden camera documented 'fly-on-the-wall' pictures of the young chicks' development, from the moment they hatched to their first attempts to flap their wings and fly.

'Isn't it marvellous?' sighed Mrs Jones, as the end credits rolled up the screen.

'Instinct,' replied Mr Jones. 'It's in the genes. It's nothing more than nature taking its course. And one day they'll have their own chicks, who'll develop exactly the same fly-the-nest instincts.'

Mrs Jones sighed again and got up to pour another cup of tea. At that moment, Jane, their 'troublesome' sixteen-year-old daughter, appeared in the doorway. Dressed in her brand new PVC miniskirt and crop top, and decorated with fluorescent make-up and recently-pierced nose, it was more than Mr Jones could cope with.

'You're not going out dressed like that!' he yelled.

'Why not?' she replied. 'Everyone wears this kind of stuff. I'll be back around midnight. Don't wait up!'

'Just one minute, young lady!' Mr Jones pulled himself out of his seat, preparing for a fight. 'No daughter of mine is going out looking like that, and that's final! Go upstairs and wash that stuff off your face right now. And that thing looks more like a wide belt than a skirt! Take it off! No, I mean . . . *stretch* it! Get a bigger one! Put something decent on! If you want to go out, you can jolly well look respectable . . . and you'll be back by ten or you won't know what's hit you! And take that thing out of your nose!'

But Jane was already half-way out of the front door, as she shouted back, 'I'll do what I want and you can't stop me!'

As Mrs Jones listened to the angry voices, she couldn't help remembering how Jane had always been such a loving girl. They'd always been such a close family. But now everything she did seemed purposely designed to offend them. And every Saturday night, the same row. Instead of snuggling up in front of the TV with them the way she used to, enjoying another in their collection of birdwatching videos, all she was interested in doing these days was going into town to do who-knows-what with her friends. Where had they gone wrong?

Where they'd gone wrong, of course, was in not learning any lessons from their birdwatching tapes. Sooner or later, Jane was obviously going to want to 'fly the nest'. But they hadn't recognised the signs early enough. So rather than working with her to prepare her for freedom, they'd left her to her instincts, with no help or guidance. In their worst moments, they'd even tried to fight against the inevitable.

Of course, it's natural for mums and dads to want to protect their children from the horrors of the outside world. It's filled with heavy traffic that might run them over, rivers and lakes they might drown in, bullies intent on intimidating them, drug dealers waiting to sell them Ecstasy, and muggers, perverts and – in the case of young ladies – young men waiting to pounce. Obviously, the safest thing to do is to shut the front door and keep them warm and secure, locked up at home. But doing this is as shortsighted and ineffective as King Canute's attempt to turn back the tide. Although Canute was a great and powerful king, there was no way he was ever going to be able to stop the tide from coming in.

One day, your children will leave home. They'll live on their own or with friends. They'll struggle to survive on too little money. They'll walk home down long, dark streets late at night. They'll choose their own friends and partners, and do what they like with them. They'll drive cars or ride motorbikes, go to parties and raves. They'll choose their own clothes, and decide for themselves whether or not to wear a coat, hat, scarf and mittens, and take a clean handkerchief. Like it or not, your control over them will be gone. So it's your task to begin work *now* to prepare them slowly for that moment.

'**When a father sets out to teach his little son to walk, he stands in front of him and holds his two hands on either side of the child, so that he cannot fall, and the boy goes toward his father between his father's hands. But the moment he is close to his father, he moves away a little and holds his hands further apart, and he does this over and over, so that the child may learn to walk.**'

The Baal Shem

Preparation is better than cure

So how do you do it? How do you prepare your kids for that fateful day when they 'fly the nest'? I have a friend who tells me that when his daughter reaches her teenage years, he plans to keep a couple of large, ferocious alsatians to protect her from 'the wrong kind of boys'. 'If they try anything, the dogs will soon sort them out!' But sadly, this strategy is doomed to failure. Sooner or later, his daughter will find a boyfriend with enough brains to bring some nice, juicy steaks to distract the dogs. Or she'll just go round to his place! And as a result, my friend will have even less influence and control over the situation than ever.

In the Middle Ages, some fathers locked up their daughters in chastity belts as a guaranteed method of ensuring their purity. And out of love, concern and even fear for our children, it's sometimes easy to wish we could do the same kind of thing today. But it wouldn't work. Even back in mediaeval days, enterprising manacled daughters ended up bedding the handsome young blacksmith's apprentice in order to get a spare key cut. Nowadays they would simply buy a Junior Hack-saw, learn how to pick the lock, or report you to Social Services!

So wise parents make it their goal to equip their children with a kind of 'internal chastity/morality/maturity belt'. In other words, they do their best to instil in them the only thing that can ultimately help and guide them – self-control.

If you're afraid of your child falling in the local river and drowning, don't keep them locked indoors – teach them how to swim! To put it another way, the question isn't *whether* to let the lead out or not, but rather *how quickly* to do this. Unfortunately there's no universal timetable. Each child is different, and some learn to handle their freedom more quickly than others.

> **'You may give them your love but not your thoughts.**
> **For they have their own thoughts.**
> **You may house their bodies but not their souls,**
> **For their souls dwell in the house of tomorrow, which**
> **You cannot visit, not even in your dreams.'**
>
> Kahlil Gibran, The Prophet

You need to prepare your kids to live their own lives

Jason lives alone. Every morning he catches the train to his job in the City, and every evening he comes back to his little suburban flat. The routine never varies. He never goes out socially, and never has friends over for dinner. He's summed up by the line from the John Mellencamp song, 'Jack And Diane': 'life goes on, long after the thrill of living is gone.' There's nothing physically wrong with him. It's just that he has no self-confidence or social skills. And the reason for this is simple: his mother, who died about ten years ago, mollycoddled and smothered him well into his forties. He never freed himself of her apron strings. And because she'd always overprotected him, he didn't know what to do or how to cope after she died. He's afraid of anything that doesn't fit his routine, because her love made her blind to the fact that she was failing to prepare him for independent living. He can cook and operate the washing machine, but he doesn't know how to make friends or take decisions. Instead of being the master of his own destiny, he's at the mercy of the future.

There was once a scientific study done into how people react to meeting someone with a serious facial disfigurement. An actress was hired to do a bogus survey in a shopping centre, and the whole thing was secretly filmed from a nearby shop. She was asked to do the same survey in four different 'roles'. *First* she had to be herself. *Then* she had to act awkwardly, without any self-confidence. *Third*, she was made up so that she looked like she had an off-putting birthmark on her face. And *finally*, with the same make-up, she again had to act awkwardly, with no self-confidence.

The results surprised even the scientists doing the experiment. The birthmark *did* make people slightly nervous, but it was the actress's social skills (her charm and self-confidence), or lack of them, that actually made all the difference. They proved to be a far bigger factor than what she looked like. The team responsible for the study concluded that people with self-confidence, self-esteem and an ability to make friends can overcome even the most severe disability. But people without these social skills – like Jason – have a disadvantage in life that has a far more negative impact than any physical disability.

So if you want your child to be truly happy and successful, you need to prepare them for what's ahead by working to develop in them the self-confidence, self-esteem, self-discipline and self-worth that are *all* vital if they're to be able to cope well with life. Beyond any shadow of doubt, it's preparation, not protection, that's the key.

> **'My father told me everything about the birds and the bees. He doesn't know anything about girls.'**
> Leopold Fechtner

Self-esteem is the key to making wise sexual choices

For example, nowhere is all this more obvious than when it comes to sex. Even the most free-wheeling and permissive parents tend to become relatively traditional when it comes to their kids and sex. It's natural for us to want to protect our children in every area of their lives, and this is doubly true in the arena of sex. Sexual decisions are the most intimate we can make. And sexual mistakes are often the most painful. In fact, it's no exaggeration to say that they can even be lethal.

But teenage sexuality is just as much a minefield for a parent as it is for their children. We want to trust our kids to make their own decisions. But we also want to keep them safe from harm. And we often find it hard to adjust to the fact that the five-year-old we used to help dress is now a sexually mature fifteen-year-old who inhabits an increasingly private world filled with their own choices.

So how *do* we provide them with that 'internal chastity belt'? Part of the answer is simply to talk to them – a prospect that sends shivers down every parent's spine. Don't worry, you're not odd. It's really quite natural to find giving 'that talk' even more embarrassing than your children find listening to it. In fact, no parent has ever talked with their child about sex without finding it a struggle at first just to get the words out . . . which, of course, is why so many parents put the whole thing off until it's too late to be of any use. But however reticent we are, the reality is that poll after poll shows children want to learn about sex initially from their parents, rather than from their friends, magazines, the TV or even their school.

So however difficult it is, it's vital to learn to discuss this important issue within the home, and to start early. There are three big mistakes to avoid:

- **Telling your kids nothing**. This only leaves the door open for their imaginations to run riot, filled with myths and half-truths picked up from elsewhere. I learnt the facts of life from my mate John Dean one wet playtime when I was ten. And that was a long time ago. These days, no child over the age of seven or eight can escape constant talk of sex. But the problem is that, without your involvement, what your kids will pick up at this age is bound to be a worrying mixture of half-truths and misunderstandings. What's more, it's all about the mechanics, with nothing about the morals. So make sure that your children get the truth from you first, and that you include information about the moral and emotional aspects of sex and sexuality, not just the mechanical and physical ones.

- **Telling your kids old wives' tales**. Just this morning, I talked to a young mum who was about four months pregnant. Her three-year-old daughter had asked her why she was getting bigger. 'What do I tell her?' she asked. That's a question most parents want answered. Stories about storks, gooseberry bushes, or birds and bees will end an embarrassing moment quickly, but in the long run just breed confusion and a lack of trust. Don't make the mistake of putting off telling your kids the truth until they're fourteen years old, saving it all up for 'the sex talk'. By then it'll be a bit too late. Start when they're three or younger by not avoiding the subject, and answering their questions as they naturally crop up. And as they get older, and can understand more, slowly make your explanations more and more detailed.

- **Telling your kids all the graphic details**. Blow-by-blow descriptions of sex make even less sense to three-year-olds than tales about storks. Too much information can be overwhelming and impossible to understand. When six-year-old John asked his mum, 'Where did I come from?', she knew the time had come, and gave him a full biological explanation of egg, ovary, orgasm and intercourse. When she'd finished, half an hour later, John's only comment was, 'That's funny. Peter says he came from Brighton!' You need to tell them the truth, but you don't need to tell them the *whole* truth *all at once*. Bit by bit will do fine. When Cornelia and I taught our kids how to tell the time, we didn't sit them down and explain in great detail everything Einstein had to say about how time is affected by motion. (One reason for this, of course, is that I don't have a clue myself!) Instead, we just told them about the big hand and the little hand and all the numbers in between. In much the same way, over the years we need slowly to explain to our children about sex. Give as much information as seems appropriate at the time, never misleading or confusing them, but also never feeling that it's your task to impart to your six-year-old the entire contents of the Kama Sutra!

Of course, it'll still be embarrassing. But isn't embarrassment better than leaving the responsibility for teaching your child about one of the most important aspects of their life to a chance conversation with someone else in the playground? If *you* get it right when they're young, *they're* far more likely to get it right when they're older.

Some parents are worried that telling their children about sex will push them into sexual relationships earlier than would otherwise be the case. They don't want to 'shatter their innocence'. But all the evidence suggests that exactly the opposite is true. As the saying goes, 'forewarned is forearmed'. Being armed with enough good information usually delays a child's sexual activity. The truth is that *innocence* is more likely to be protected when *ignorance* is removed. Why? Well, quite simply, your openness and honesty will allow them to make better, more informed, more mature and more responsible choices. Coping with their newly-activated hormones is difficult enough, but doing so without any guidance makes it even tougher.

Most of the 8,000 under-sixteens who become pregnant every year in the UK never even wanted to have sex, let alone a baby. According to the Family Planning Association, most of them say they 'just got carried away'. In other words, they had sex without ever really deciding to. And the main reason why young people allow themselves to be swept along in the heat of passion? 'I just didn't know how to say "No".'

Added to this, most young people – like most adults – desperately need to feel loved and accepted. In fact, more than 80 per cent of teenagers aren't happy with the way they look. Their nose, their hair, their height, their weight, their glasses, their zits . . . or the whole lot. As a result, they're frantically searching for some kind of reassurance that they're valuable. This can mean that they're more likely to have sex out of a desire to *be* loved than because they're necessarily *in* love. In fact, recent research has shown that stable, secure, self-confident teenagers are far less promiscuous than their insecure counterparts.

Information and education are vitally important. But they're not enough on their own. Sooner or later, your kids will make their own decisions about when, where and with whom they have sex. If you want these decisions to be informed and responsible, it's your job to do all you can to help them to feel good about themselves, as well as making sure they're well educated on the subject. Otherwise, they'll be open to all sorts of emotional arm-twisting.

> **'Dad, now that I'm fourteen, can I wear silk stockings and a brassiere?' 'No, Derek. You can't.'**
>
> Anonymous

Trust breeds trustworthiness

Self-confidence and self-discipline develop as you're slowly willing to grant your children greater and greater levels of responsibility, and the freedom that goes with it. This is the best way a parent has of saying, 'I trust you'. If you don't do this, your child will never *feel* trusted or trustworthy. And that means they're unlikely to *become* trustworthy.

Peter and Janice recently told me about the first time they let their two daughters – aged seven and nine – walk to school on their own. The experiment was a total disaster. Janice had told them that she'd be following about twenty metres behind, just in case. And because they knew she was behind, and wouldn't let anything bad happen to them, they didn't take things seriously. In fact, they paid so little attention to road safety that it was a wonder they didn't get run over. But rather than calling the whole experiment off, Janice told the girls they were now ready to go to school *entirely* on their own the next day. She secretly followed them anyway, of course, but this time made sure they never suspected she was there. The two girls couldn't have done better. Thinking they were alone, they acted quite differently. They held hands, walked sensibly, and stopped, looked and listened where they were *meant* to stop, look and listen. Entrusted with the task of looking after themselves, they behaved responsibly and with perfect care.

> **'A father is a banker provided by nature.'**
>
> Anonymous

One size doesn't fit all, so treat your kids as individuals

The big question is, 'What's the right speed at which to grant freedom, to trust and to let go?' It's all a bit like teaching your child to ride a two-wheeler. You start by promising not to let go of the saddle, running alongside them as they get the feel of it. Then, when they're confident enough, you let go – just for a second or two to start with. Eventually, when they're able to go short distances on their own, you let go for longer periods, still running alongside just in case. It's what every parent does, but even so, it's still different every time because each child is unique. For example, our first daughter, Emily, learnt to ride a two-wheeler in ten minutes flat, while our elder son, Daniel, took several weeks to achieve the same thing.

Just as with learning to ride a bike, there's no universal timescale for letting your kids go and giving them responsibility and freedom. Each child responds to love, freedom, discipline and instruction in different ways. Some need more guidance, others less. And this means that treating each child *fairly* isn't the same thing as treating them all *the same*. In our house, for instance, if we let our kids set their own bedtimes, our girls would always go to bed at a reasonable time. Our boys, on the other hand, would never voluntarily enter their bedrooms. They'd both wake up tired, late and stiff the next morning, still in front of the TV in the living-room. This has nothing to do with their ages, and everything to do with their characters.

The parent who's looking for a list of *dos* and *don'ts*, and a firm timetable for letting go, is the kind of parent who'd make big mistakes even if such timetables were available. In order to work out when to keep your kids on a tight lead and when to let go, you need to spend time getting to know each of them very well indeed. There's no alternative and no short cut to this. You have to make time to get to know their wants and needs, their strengths and weaknesses, and their unique ways of seeing the world. If you don't, you'll simply end up reacting to their behaviour in a non-constructive way rather than thoughtfully working to shape it with them.

> **'You are the bows from which your children as living arrows are sent forth.'**
>
> Kahlil Gibran, *The Prophet*

Delegation: the art of parenting

The art of delegation is the art of knowing when to move from a strict set of rules to ever greater degrees of trust and responsibility. And the better you know your child, the more able you are to make good judgments about how and when to do this. Too much responsibility too soon can be totally overwhelming, but too little will always leave them believing you don't trust them.

Pocket money is a good example of delegation, because it allows you to give your children some responsibility for buying the things they want or need. Through it, you grant them limited control over their finances, and begin to teach them the budgeting skills they'll need later in life. Added to this, giving your teenage kids a limited budget to choose and buy their own clothes is a further way of creating trust, and helping them learn to handle money wisely.

It's vital to understand that delegation is *not* about just washing your hands of responsibility. Some people see it as a way of passing the buck. But that's not delegation – it's dumping! In my job as the director of a charity, I delegate huge amounts of work. But this doesn't mean I'm no longer responsible for it.

Though the work is entrusted to others, it's my job to make sure that they're getting all the backup, support and guidance they need. If things are going badly, it's just as much my fault as anyone else's. Delegation is about *sharing* responsibility with others, not dumping it on them. *They* are responsible for the details, but you are responsible for *them*. And if they have too much responsibility to handle, or too little to inspire them, you haven't delegated well.

DELEGATION IS THE ART OF PARENTING... YOUR MUM TOLD ME TO TELL YOU.

So as a mum or dad, you still remain ultimately responsible for all the things you delegate to your children, and therefore for checking how they're getting on. Rather than blaming them and giving up when things are going wrong, you need to tweak the system a little bit by adjusting the level of responsibility given.

Delegation can be extremely frustrating. When you first teach someone to do something, there are bound to be 'teething problems'. Mistakes are inevitable when you're learning something new. It's at this point that you face the temptation to take the reins back and do it yourself. But trusting someone with a task and then taking it away again is like saying that you've realised they're not trustworthy, and the end result will be worse than what you started with.

So it's important to know your child, think about the appropriate level of responsibility to delegate to them, keep your cool when the problems inevitably occur, encourage them by pointing out what they did *right*, and urge them to try again when they fail. This way, they'll slowly grow in confidence, expertise and – because they feel *trusted* – *trustworthiness*.

You won't always be there for your children. One day they'll leave home, whether you've helped to get them ready for it or not. So preparation is the key. Grasp the opportunity you have to help prepare them *today*!

Remember

- Your children will eventually fly the nest: it's instinctive and good.
- If you don't prepare them for independence, who will?
- If you over-protect your children, they will never be able to cope alone.
- Self-esteem is key for making the right choices in sex and other areas.
- Children need to be trusted in order to become trustworthy.
- Too much responsibility will crush your child, too little will stunt their growth into maturity.
- Each child is different: there's no universal formula for letting go.
- Delegation is the art of parenting: helping your children to help themselves.

Key principles

Prove to your kids TODAY that you trust them.

How to achieve it

- Think of some responsibility you can give to your child.
- Plan how to support them in this responsibility, but never take it from them.
- Praise your kids when they behave responsibly.
- Talk with your kids about the big decisions in their lives.

Be Wise

Ten things you should, and should *not*, say to your kids

'If it's not one thing, it's a mother!'

Lorraine Ingham

'Sticks and stones...'

'Sticks and stones may break my bones, but words will never hurt me!' Perhaps the most inaccurate of all old sayings. The truth is so very different. Sticks and stones can hurt all right, but even then it's usually the emotional injuries that stay with you long after any physical ones have healed. Words have enormous power – for good or ill, positive or negative. We can use them as weapons or use them to heal. So it's vitally important for us to do all we can to reduce to a minimum the put-downs we let slip out, and at the same time work at making it a habit to say things that reinforce the principles we've looked at throughout this book. In this chapter, we take a look at ten of the worst, and then ten of the best, things you can say to your children.

Every child is born with the inbuilt ability to drive his or her parents crazy. As a result, from time to time we find ourselves blurting out all kinds of things we don't really mean, and then regretting them – sometimes even before they've finished leaving our mouths.

We all send messages we regret. And we wish we could take

[1] Tip Ten is adapted from Michele Elliot's book *501 Ways to be a Good Parent* published by Hodder & Stoughton.

them back, but we can't. Of course, the very good news is that the occasional unkind or unthoughtful remark isn't going to wound your child permanently. But it's equally true that if we allow these same comments to become a way of life, then there's a real danger that our children will be seriously hurt by them.

We usually make hurtful remarks because we're angry or frustrated. And though most of the time we don't mean what we say, the impact of our words can still be devastating, destroying confidence and trust and leaving their 'victim' with a sense of bewilderment and inadequacy.

> **'It never occurs to a boy that he will some day be as dumb as his father.'**
>
> Laurence J. Peter

Ten of the worst

1 'You're so stupid!'

We've all done it. It's been a hard day, and you're exhausted. The phone hasn't stopped ringing since you got home, and the kids have demanded almost all of your energy and attention. All you want to do is collapse in front of the TV and watch something totally mindless before going to bed. But as you put them to bed, you almost fall over your son's toy, left carelessly on the stairs. 'You stupid boy!' you shout, 'I could have broken my neck!'

We all gain our understanding of ourselves from those around us, especially our parents. So if you tell your kids they're stupid, they're likely to believe you, which is guaranteed gradually to eat away at their self-esteem and self-confidence. And a lack of self-esteem and self-confidence means that, rather than being armed with the resources they'll need to make the most of life, your kids will struggle to realise their full potential. So be careful always to differentiate between the *act* and the *child*, and next time your kid leaves their toy car on the stairs for you to trip over, tell them it was a stupid thing to do, but *never* tell them they're stupid for doing it.

> **'Literature is mostly about having sex and not much about having children; life is the other way round.'**
>
> David Lodge

2 'Sometimes, I wish you'd never been born!'

This is the ultimate put-down. It's the same as saying, 'I wish you didn't even exist.' Once again, it's an easy thing to say. You're frustrated and exhausted, and you've had about all you can take, but there's never a time when you can just 'clock off'. You're a parent twenty-four hours a day. Of course, once you've calmed down, you realise that you don't actually mean it, but your kids don't know that. They depend so heavily on your love and acceptance. So if you don't want them, who does? What are they worth?

We all say things we don't mean. But if it's hard enough for us as adults to accept that other adults don't always mean what they say to us, it's a whole lot harder still for kids.

> **'That all men should be brothers is the dream of people who have no brothers.'**
>
> Charles Chincolles, *Pensées de Tout le Monde*

3 'If only you were more like your brother!'

Each child is different. They have their own distinct personalities, complete with their own set of strengths and weaknesses. So by telling them to behave more like their brother or sister, or the Clarke kids next door, the message we're sending them is that they're not good enough as they are, and that we'd love them more if they were someone else. In the long run, they'll end up not liking themselves, and probably whoever it is you're comparing them with as well.

As parents, it's our job to love our children unconditionally, even when we don't feel like it. And anyway, comparing a child with their brother or sister is totally counter-productive. It won't encourage them to do better. It will only sap what remains of their self-esteem and drain them of the confidence or desire to succeed. It's a sure way to cripple them, not liberate them. Instead, talk to them about specific areas of their lives in which you'd like to see improvements without comparing them with anyone else. And make sure that your love for them is never seen as being based on their performance. Love them for who they are, not what they do.

> **'This boy has strange ways, and he'll probably end up there.'**
>
> Ampleforth on Angus Loughran

4 'You could do so well, if only . . .'

Children need to build on their strengths as well as improve their weaknesses. But when you tell them that they could do well *if only*, you're effectively saying both that their strengths aren't noticeable and that their weaknesses are too great. So, as with comparing them with other people, even though you think you're giving them advice that will motivate them and help them to get better, what you're actually doing is the opposite: you're making it far harder for them to improve. Unless they know what they're doing right, they won't know what strengths they have to build on.

Negative messages wear people down, and destroy confidence. So catch your kids doing something right and praise them for it, or they'll never develop the kind of confidence in their abilities they'll need if they're to tackle their weaknesses and learn to hear criticism constructively.

> **'Do you have a happy family? Or are the kids still at home?'**
>
> Anonymous

5 'Look at everything I've given up for you!'

It's easy to see the costs of being a parent: emotional, physical, financial, etc. There are times when every parent wonders if all they are for their kids is an automatic meal-machine, cash dispenser and taxi service all rolled into one, with no thanks or obvious appreciation. Is it really worth all the hard work and sacrifice? In a moment of self-pity, out it comes: 'If it hadn't been for you, I could have . . .'

Once again, a *short* sentence with a *massive*, guilt-enducing, insecurity-building impact. Your kids didn't ask to be born, so from the moment they come into the world, you owe them everything. But you're not alone. *Every* parent has to give things up for their children, and always will. It's the cost of being a parent. So sacrifice isn't something we should expect any thanks for: it's just part of the job description.

> 'The illusions of childhood are necessary experiences. A child should not be denied a balloon because an adult knows that sooner or later it will burst.'
>
> Marcelene Cox

6 'Act your age!'

Few ten-year-olds can tell you the square root of 264, and there's no reason why they should be able to. Usually, when we tell our kids to act their age, what we really mean is, '*Don't* act your age!' But this just isn't fair. Your child can't act older than their years or experience of life will allow them to. Most of the time, it's precisely because they're acting their age that we find their behaviour so irritating or frustrating.

What's needed here isn't genius on the part of the child, but more patience on the part of the adult. No one comes out of the womb already able to behave with approved etiquette for tea at Buckingham Palace, or able to understand the *Daily Telegraph*. More to the point, they don't come with the wisdom and experience to behave like adults when they're not. So perhaps it's we parents who should act our age a bit more. Rather than expecting our kids to be more mature than their years, we should allow them the chance to mature in their own time, like a fine wine.

> 'The first half of our lives is ruined by our parents, and the second by our children.'
>
> Clarence Darrow

7 'Don't be silly, there's nothing to be frightened of!'

Like 'Act your age', this is one of those things that demands too much too soon. Kids have very active imaginations. Most adults don't enjoy walking alone down a dark alley in a rough neighbourhood, or sleeping in their own house after it's been burgled. But most children get scared by things that most adults, because of their maturity and experience of life, don't find even remotely chilling; like spiders, or the dark, or shadows, etc.

Part of being a child is learning how to use your imagination. But sometimes your imagination just gets the better of you. There's no real difference between you dropping your popcorn and jumping six feet in the air during *Alien* or *The Silence of the Lambs*, and them hiding behind the sofa during *The Lion King* or the infamous childcatcher scenes in *Chitty Chitty Bang Bang*. Comfort and inform your child, but never tell them they're silly or laugh at them. Teach them that it's OK to be scared, and to admit to it when they are. Otherwise they'll be so afraid of what you might say that they'll just suffer in silence, and never come to you with their fears.

> **'A father is someone we can look up to no matter how tall we get.'**
>
> Anonymous

8 'Wait until your father gets home!'

In Victorian times, 'Wait until your father gets home!' was the ultimate threat. So I suppose that in these days of equality, the words, 'Wait until your mother gets home!' should strike just as much terror into the hearts of boys and girls everywhere. It may seem like an effective tactic – 'good cop, bad cop' – but dumping the burden of discipline for 'serious' offences on to one parent is actually a recipe for disaster. It just reinforces stereotyped ideas about the different roles of men and women in the family. It makes the father look like an awful tyrant, and rather than making the mother look good, it presents her as being weak. It's like saying, 'I don't have the authority or the stomach to discipline you.' As a result, it eats away at the respect children have for both their mother and father.

Fair discipline is always best administered by the parent who was there when the 'crime' took place. So don't dump *your* problems on to your partner in a situation they know nothing about. Don't load a gun and then expect *them* to fire it. If it's serious, and you need time to calm down and think before you act, say something like, 'I'm going to discipline you for this, but I want to be fair. So your father and I will talk about it later, and then I'll decide.'

> **'Nobody is so clever that he knows what he is doing all the time.'**
>
> John Irving

9 'You have no idea what you're talking about!'

It was IBM who dismissed the commercial concept of the computer when it was first presented to them, claiming it would never catch on! And John Lennon's Aunt Mimi is famous for having warned him, 'A guitar's all right, John, but you'll never make a living out of it!' With hindsight, of course, neither IBM nor Aunt Mimi could have got it more wrong. But the truth is that, years from now, people will laugh at some of the things *we* say and believe. It's only natural. After all, even we cringe at some of the opinions we held when we were younger, not to mention the clothes we wore! If you've kept any of the things you wrote as a child – maybe a diary or a school essay – you'll see just how naïve you were back then. All of us say daft things from time to time. And your children are no different. They try on their knowledge for size, talking confidently about things they really know very little about.

So be sensitive in the way you handle them. You'll inevitably have to correct them sometimes, but be very careful about how you go about this task. Don't humiliate or embarrass them, or put them down. You don't want them to lose confidence in themselves, even when they're wrong. Instead, build on what they've got right. Show respect for their views, and from there gently help them to see where they've gone wrong: 'That's interesting, but what do you think about . . . ?'

'How many millions of times have I told you not to exaggerate?'

Father to small boy

10 'You always/never...'

When they're irritated, people often fall into the habit of generalising their attacks on others. So 'You forgot to put the toilet seat down last night' becomes 'You *never* put the toilet seat down'. A specific criticism points out a particular mistake, giving the child concerned the opportunity to address the problem. But a generalised criticism feels like an attack on their character. 'You *always* . . .' or 'You *never* . . .' is like saying 'You're inadequate'. And as a parent, this is something you don't want to do. After all, if your child really is inadequate, it's probably inherited! What's more, to say that someone *never* tells the truth, or thinks of others, is almost certainly not true. So you're only giving them a reason to reject what you say, and get upset or angry about it, rather than learn anything from it.

So be *specific* about what your child has done wrong. Generalised attacks or criticism are likely just to make them lose heart and give up. Rather than saying, 'You never do your homework on time,' be specific: 'You didn't do your maths homework on time last week.' And how about offering some practical help or advice on getting themselves organised enough to do it on time this week?

'Every child should be able to enjoy working, knowing they're loved. They shouldn't have to endure the struggle of working in order to feel loved.'

Cornelia Chalke

Ten of the best

Praise is the miracle tool. Words can help your children to blossom and flourish, or cause their self-confidence to shrivel and die. So work at constantly sending your children lots of encouraging, supportive and positive messages about who they are and how they're doing. Remember that 'What you *say* is what you get'. If you reinforce your kids' good points, they'll work on them. But if you spend your time drawing attention to their mistakes, you're leaving them with no positive guidance.

1 'I'm so proud of you, well done!'

Children need constant encouragement if they're going to build the confidence they require to be at peace with themselves and make a success of their lives. They need to know that they're valued for who they are. They also need to be praised for what they've done and the effort they've made. So catch your kids 'red-handed' doing something right and praise them for it. Be specific: let them know you're proud of them – it's a great way to build up their self-esteem. If they know you're proud of them, it will help them develop a healthy self-respect. And if you're specific with your praise, you'll also help them to identify what they're good at.

> **'Parents learn a lot from their children about coping with life.'**
>
> Muriel Spark

2 'You're so thoughtful . . .'

We all repeat behaviour that gets us a positive response, and your children are no different. So you can play a major role in helping them to develop as thoughtful, caring, kind, honest, considerate and sensitive individuals. You shape your kids through your example, but also through the comments you make. So when you see your child behaving in a way you're proud of, let them know. Again, be specific. Comments such as, 'You're so honest . . . thank you,' will not only make your child feel loved and appreciated, but is almost guaranteed to lead them to act in the same way on future occasions. Remember the 'Law of Reinforcement': we repeat behaviour if we're praised for it.

> **'It's what you listen to when you're growing up that you always come back to.'**
>
> Al Cohn

3 'You're clever to have worked that out!'

Children, like adults, tend to enjoy doing things they're good at. They're also more likely to become good at doing things they enjoy. So by praising your kids for using their initiative and thinking things through, you're encouraging them to think about things even more in the future. They'll begin to see learning as something enjoyable. By using this kind of statement, you're doing far more than just telling them they were clever on one particular occasion. You're also helping them to develop the incentive to fulfil even more of their potential in the future. (And if they didn't manage to work it out, praise them for the effort they put in anyway: 'Well done, you really tried hard. I'm proud of what you did.')

> **'I do not love him because he is good, but because he is my little child.'**
>
> Rabindranath Tagore

4 'I love you.'

This is the most important thing you can ever say to your child. Perhaps the best phrase in the English language. And there's no reason to use it sparingly. But it's not enough just to say it, of course: you have to prove it's true by what you do. As parents, you're the most important people in your children's lives. Knowing that you love them totally, with no strings attached, is the foundation on which they'll build their entire future. If that foundation isn't strong and sure, it might not survive life's storms. But if your kids know that you love them – and that you always will, no matter what – they'll develop a positive self-image and, as a result, will be able to endure whatever life throws at them.

MUMMY LOVES YOU VERY MUCH...

THANKS FOR NOT KEEPING MUM ABOUT IT!

And not just endure, but enjoy. Because if your kids know you love them, they'll be able to love other people better. It was Jesus who said, 'Love others as you love *yourself*'. In other words, if you haven't got a good self-image and learnt to 'love yourself', it will be extremely hard to love other people. You can't love others as you should until you've learnt to love yourself a little first. The truth is that the quality of love you show your children will affect not just how well they cope with life, but the depth of their relationships with others. So be generous with these three little words and back them up with plenty of proof that you're telling the truth.

> **'The first five years of a child's life is a period of rapid change. In this time a parent can age twenty years!'**
>
> Anonymous

5 'What do you think about . . . ?'

This is the kind of open question that encourages your child to talk. By using it, you're teaching them how to think about and express their views, and how to hold a conversation. If you love someone, you value their opinion, even when you disagree with it. In this way you reinforce the message that you like them, respect them, enjoy their company, and find their conversation thought-provoking. That's why engaged couples spend hours on end discussing things like what colour to paint the bathroom in their first flat. They're keen to know each other's deepest thoughts about almost everything.

Many parents and children don't really talk. They just grunt at each other like cavemen. Asking kids for their opinion is a way of telling them that it matters to you what they think. And that means that you value not just their opinion, but *them*. Parents often complain that their kids don't talk to them, but it's their job to encourage it. And there's no better time to start than now.

> **'Instead of getting hard ourselves and trying to compete, women should try and give their best qualities to men – bring them softness, teach them how to cry.'**
>
> Joan Baez

6 'It's OK to cry.'

Everyone hurts and everyone cries. It's vital for your children to learn that it's OK to express their fears and emotions rather than bottling them up, where all they can do is eat away at them from the inside. It's a tragedy that so many British men, for instance, can't talk honestly and openly about the way they feel. 'Real men don't cry,' they were taught. But this terrible advice leaves people isolated and unable to express themselves and their feelings. They can't even grieve. Bottled up emotion leads at best to frustration, and at worst to violence. By teaching your kids to express their grief or fear, by saying and showing that it's OK to cry, you help them to face these emotions head on and deal with them. You also teach them that help is always available if and when they need it.

> **'Ability is not all there is – a good athlete is not always a winning athlete.'**
>
> George Allen

7 'You tried your best, and that's what counts.'

The odds are against your child becoming a World Champion at anything. Most of us are pretty mediocre when it comes to great achievements, and excel at things that don't make the headlines. But however intellectually, athletically, musically or artistically gifted they might be, no one can be a World Champion at *everything*. So it's very important to teach your children that doing *their* best matters more in the long run than doing *the* best. After all, no world record lasts forever. Sooner or later, even a World Champion becomes a Former World Champion. The only way your children will ever find peace within themselves is by truly understanding the Olympic motto: 'It's not the winning, but the taking part.' And the only way to make sure they're convinced of this is to keep telling them.

> **'The fundamental defect with fathers is that they want their children to be a credit to them.'**
>
> Bertrand Russell

8 'It's OK to make mistakes.'

Everyone makes mistakes. So if they're to learn how to cope with failure – either their own or someone else's – your kids will need to know that making a mistake doesn't make them a bad person. It just makes them human. You need to reassure them that making a mistake isn't the end of the world, and that you still love them. That way, they'll have the self-worth they need to learn positive lessons from their failures, so they're prepared for the knocks and setbacks that life is bound to bring them. They'll also have the self-confidence necessary to own up to their mistakes and take responsibility for them in the future, as well as having the generosity to deal kindly and forgivingly with those whose mistakes inconvenience them.

> **'My father is in a bad mood. This means he is feeling better.'**
>
> Adrian Mole in Sue Townsend's
> *The Secret Diary of Adrian Mole*

9 'I'm sorry. Will you forgive me?'

Admitting that *you* make mistakes is just as important as showing your kids that *they're* 'allowed' to make them. In fact, it's the other half of the equation. You'll never convince them that it's acceptable to make mistakes if you're never prepared to admit to yours. By admitting when you're wrong, you show that it's OK to be honest about yourself, and you set an example for your children to follow when they mess up. By asking their forgiveness when you've hurt them, you also show that you love and respect them, and care about what they think of you.

> **'Your father is a great man, whether or not he's a worldly success. He's someone you can look up to. He helps shape your worldview, dispenses**

discipline, teaches object lessons, hands down material and moral legacies.'

John Winokur in *Fathers*

10 'I said NO!'

Your child must learn to live within boundaries: to understand and respect the difference between right and wrong, between what's acceptable and what isn't. And it's your job to teach them. If *you* don't impose boundaries on their behaviour, sooner or later someone else will. And you can bet that it'll hurt a lot more then than it would coming from you now. So don't think that by giving in to your child when they throw a tantrum in the supermarket or at mealtimes, you're making life easier either for you or for them. The fact is that you're actually just storing up trouble for later on, and no one's going to thank you for it . . . especially them! If you don't quietly and firmly teach your son or daughter when they're still young that 'No' means just that, you're headed for difficult times in future years. And you won't be doing them, or the rest of society, any favours.

The Adventure Continues . . .

> 'Those who don't learn from the past are condemned to repeat it.'
>
> Attributed to George Santayana

I've tried hard to make this book as practical and down-to-earth as possible. If I had to summarise its basic message in one page, I'd say that a successful parent is one who:

- Trusts their own judgment, but never stops learning.
- Shows their children they're valuable by making time for them.
- Gives their kids self-esteem by showing that they love them unconditionally.
- Gives their children self-discipline by disciplining them in a disciplined way.
- Builds up their children's self-worth by praising them for what they do right.
- Teaches their kids right from wrong by being a responsible role model.
- Gives their kids freedom within safe limits by making and enforcing reasonable family rules.
- Teaches their children fairness by apologising when they're in the wrong.
- Prepares their kids for independent living by delegating responsibility to them.

Remember: you can't be a perfect parent, but you can be a really *successful* one – one that your kids are proud of. It takes time, hard work and a lot of persistence, but if you're prepared to put in the effort, it's the most worthwhile and rewarding task in the world. In fact, as one of my friends puts it, 'It's a gas!'

Alfred Nobel, the nineteenth-century explosives genius who invented nitroglycerine, detonators, dynamite and gelignite, never did like himself very much. But the wealthy Swedish industrialist liked himself even less one morning in 1888 when he found himself reading his own obituary in the newspaper. A careless journalist had got him mixed up with his brother, who had recently died, and so Nobel had the rare privilege of seeing himself as the world saw him – a multi-millionaire recluse who had amassed his wealth from the making of weapons.

Nobel, who had invented his explosives for peaceful use in mining and road-building, had long been troubled by their military uses. He was determined this was not how he wanted to be remembered. So he set about changing his will to ensure that, when he died, his vast fortune would go to fund the prizes that bear his name in physics, chemistry, medicine, literature and, most importantly of all, peace.

One day, our children will sum up our lives in the same way as that journalist did Alfred Nobel's. They may not write it down, or even verbalise it, but our obituary will be written on their hearts. So the question is: How will your children remember you?

One of the prayers I pray most often is simply this: 'Dear Lord, thank you for my children and the privilege of being their dad. Help me to make a good job of being someone they can really be proud of.' Most parents pray from time to time, but many wait until it's an emergency and make a kind of 999 call. Me? I take all the help I can get. How about you?

Further Information

Organisations

Parentalk
PO Box 23142
London SE1 OZT

Tel: 020 7450 9073
Fax: 020 7450 9060
e-mail: info@parentalk.co.uk
Website: www.parentalk.co.uk

Provides a range of resources and services designed to inspire parents to enjoy parenthood.

Care for the Family
PO Box 488
Cardiff CF15 7YY

Tel: 029 2081 0800
Fax: 029 2081 4089
e-mail: mail@cff.org.uk
Website: www.care-for-the-family.org.uk

Provides support for families through seminars, resources and special projects.

Child Benefit Centre
Department for Work and Pensions
Child Benefit Centre (Washington)
PO Box 1
Newcastle-upon-Tyne NE88 1AA

Tel: 0870 155 5540
e-mail: child-benefit@dwp.gsi.gov.uk
Website: www.dwp.gov.uk

Administers all child benefits claims.

Child Support Agency
PO Box 55
Brierley Hill
West Midlands DY5 1YL
Tel: 08457 133133 (enquiry line)/08457 138924 (for those who
are hard of hearing)

In Northern Ireland:
Great Northern Tower
17 Great Victoria Street
Belfast BT2 7AD
Tel: 08457 139896

*The Government agency that assesses maintenance levels for
parents who no longer live with their children.*

Childalert
e-mail: info@childalert.co.uk
Website: www.childalert.co.uk

*Childalert is an information service for parents and anyone else
looking after children. It provides information about child safety
and wellbeing in the home and on the move, covering pre-
conception to the first weeks at home, to the energy and
determination of toddlers, to the concerns of raising boys and
girls and how different they can be.*

Children 1st
83 Whitehouse Loan
Edinburgh EH9 1AT

Tel: 0131 446 2300
Fax: 0131 446 2339
e-mail: info@children1st.org.uk
Website: www.children1st.org.uk

A national Scottish voluntary organisation providing advice and support to parents on the care and protection of their children.

Citizens' Advice Bureau (CAB)
Website: www.nacab.org.uk

A free and confidential service giving information and advice on topics such as benefits; maternity rights; debts; housing, consumer, employment and legal problems; family and personal difficulties. It also has details of useful national and local organisations. Ask at your local library or look in your phone book for your nearest office. Opening times may vary.

Contact-A-Family
209–211 City Road
London EC1V 1JN

Helpline: 0808 808 3555
Tel: 020 7608 8700
Fax: 020 7608 8701
e-mail: info@cafamily.org.uk
Website: www.cafamily.org.uk

Brings together families whose children have disabilities.

Council for Disabled Children
8 Wakley Street
London EC1V 7QE

Tel: 020 7843 6000
Fax: 020 7278 9512
e-mail: jkhan@ncb.org.uk
Website: www.ncb.org.uk

Provides an information and advice service on all matters relating to disability for children and their families.

Couple Counselling Scotland
18 York Place
Edinburgh EH1 3EP

Tel: 0131 558 9669
Fax: 0131 556 6596

Provides a confidential counselling service for relationship problems of any kind.

Credit Action
6 Regent Terrace
Cambridge CB2 1AA

Helpline: 0800 591084
Tel: 01223 324034
Website: www.creditaction.com

The National Money Education Charity that promotes self-help in money education matters. Practical, sensitive and confidential advice on debt management is available via the freephone helpline. Also, a free self-help guide will be sent where appropriate. The money guide section has a good self-help guide to dealing with personal debt.

Dads & Lads

YMCA England National Dads & Lads Project
Dee Bridge House
25–27 Lower Bridge Street
Chester CH1 1RS

Tel: 01244 403090
e-mail: dirk@parenting.ymca.org.uk
ahowie@themail.co.uk

Locally based projects run jointly by YMCA and Care for the Family for fathers and sons, mentors and boys. They offer a unique opportunity to get together with other fathers and sons for a game of football and other activities. To find out where your nearest Dads & Lads project is based or to get help starting a new one, please contact Dirk Uitterdijk at the above address.

Daycare Trust

21 St George's Road
London SE1 6ES

Tel: 020 7840 3350
Website: www.daycaretrust.org.uk

Gives free advice to parents on childcare issues, promotes affordable childcare and helps you to decide what type of childcare might suit your child and family circumstances.

Fathers Direct

Herald House
Lambs Passage
Bunhill Row
London EC1Y 8TQ

Tel: 020 7920 9491
Fax: 020 7374 2966
e-mail: enquiries@fathersdirect.com

Website: www.fathersdirect.com

An information resource for fathers.

Gingerbread
7 Sovereign Close
Sovereign Court
London E1W 3HW

Advice line: 0800 018 4318 (Mon–Fri 9 a.m.–5 p.m.)
Tel: 020 7488 9300
Fax: 020 7488 9333
e-mail: office@gingerbread.org.uk
Website: www.gingerbread.org.uk

Provides day-to-day support and practical help for lone parents.

Health Development Agency
Holborn Gate,
330 High Holborn
London WC1 7BA

Tel: 020 7430 0850
Publications line: 01235 465565
Fax: 020 7061 3390
e-mail: communications@had-online.org.uk
Website: www.had-online.org.uk

Produces a wide range of leaflets and other useful information for families on a wide variety of topics.

Home-Start UK
2 Salisbury Road
Leicester LE1 7QR
Tel: 0116 233 9955
Fax: 0116 233 0232
e-mail: info@home-start.org.uk
Website: www.home-start.org.uk

In Northern Ireland:
133 Bloomfield Avenue
Belfast BT5
Tel/fax: 028 9046 0772
e-mail: heather.knox@homestartni.vo.uk

Volunteers offer support, friendship and practical help to young families in their own homes.

Meet-A-Mum Association (MAMA)
Waterside Centre
26 Avenue Road
London SE25 4DX

Helpline: 020 8768 0123 (Mon–Fri 7–10 p.m.)
Tel: 020 8771 5595
e-mail: meet-a-mum.assoc@blueyonder.co.uk
Website: www.mama.org.uk

Provides counselling, practical support and group therapy for women suffering from post-natal depression.

National Autistic Society
393 City Road
London EC1V 1NG

Autism helpline: 0870 600 8585 (Mon–Fri 10 a.m.–4 p.m.)
Tel: 020 7833 2299
Fax: 020 7833 9666
e-mail: nas@nas.org.uk
          autismhelpline@nas.org.uk
Website: www.nas.org.uk

Exists to champion the rights and interests of all people with autism and to ensure that they and their families receive quality services appropriate to their needs.

National Childminding Association
8 Masons Hill
Bromley
Kent BR2 9EY

Advice line: 0800 169 4486 (Mon, Tues & Thurs 10 a.m.–12 &
  2–4 p.m.; Fri 2–4 p.m.)
Tel: 020 8464 6164
Fax: 020 8290 6834
e-mail: info@ncma.org.uk
Website: www.ncma.org.uk

Informs childminders, parents and employers about the best practices in childminding.

National Council for One Parent Families
255 Kentish Town Road
London NW5 2LX

Lone Parent Line: 0800 018 5026 (Mon–Fri 9.15 a.m.–5.15 p.m.)
Maintenance & Money Line: 020 7428 5424 (Mon & Thurs 11
  a.m.–2 p.m.; Tues 3–6 p.m.)
General enquiries: 020 7428 5400
Fax: 020 7482 4851
e-mail: info@oneparentfamilies.org.uk
Website: www.oneparentfamilies.org.uk

An information service for lone parents.

National Eczema Society
Hill House
Highgate Hill
London N19 5NA

Information line: 0870 241 3604 (weekdays 1–4 p.m.)
General enquiries tel: 020 7281 3553
Website: www.eczema.org

*The National Eczema Society is the only charity in the UK
dedicated to providing support and information for people with
eczema and their carers.*

National Family and Parenting Institute
430 Highgate Studios
53–79 Highgate Road
London NW5 1TL

Tel: 020 7424 3460
Fax: 020 7485 3590
e-mail: info@nfpi.org
Website: www.nfpi.org

*An independent charity set up to provide a strong national focus
on parenting and families in the twenty-first century.*

National NEWPIN (New Parent and Infant Network)
Sutherland House
35 Sutherland Square
Walworth
London SE17 3EE

Tel: 020 7358 5900
Fax: 020 7701 2660
e-mail: info@newpin.org.uk
Website: www.newpin.org.uk

*A network of local centres offering a range of services for parents
and children.*

NHS Direct
Advice line: 0845 4647
Website: www.nhsdirect.co.uk

NIPPA (The early years organisation)
6C Wildflower Way
Apollo Road
Belfast BT12 6TA

Tel: 028 9066 2825
Fax: 028 9038 1270
e-mail: mail@nippa.org
Website: www.nippa.org

Promotes high-quality early childhood care and education services.

NSPCC
Weston House
42 Curtain Road
London EC2A 3NH

Helpline: 0800 800 5000
Tel: 020 7825 2500
Fax: 020 7825 2525
Website: www.nspcc.org.uk

Aims to prevent child abuse and neglect in all its forms and give practical help to families with children at risk. The NSPCC also produces leaflets with information and advice on positive parenting – for these, call 020 7825 2500.

One Parent Families Scotland

13 Gayfield Square
Edinburgh EH1 3NX

Tel: 0131 556 3899
Fax: 0131 557 7899
e-mail: info@opfs.org.uk
Website: www.ofps.org.uk

Provides information, training, counselling and support to one parent families throughout Scotland.

Oneplusone

The Wells
7/15 Rosebery Avenue
London EC1R 4SP

Tel: 020 7841 3660
Fax: 020 7841 3670
e-mail: info@oneplusone.org.uk
Website: www.oneplusone.org.uk

Aims to build through research a framework for understanding contemporary marriage and partnership.

Parenting Education and Support Forum

Unit 431 Highgate Studios
53–79 Highgate Road
London NW5 1TL

Tel: 020 7284 8370
Fax: 020 7485 3587
e-mail: pesf@dial.pipex.com
Website: www.parenting-forum.org.uk

Aims to raise awareness of the importance of parenting and its impact on all aspects of child development.

Parentline Plus
520 Highgate Studios
53–76 Highgate Road
Kentish Town
London NW5 1TL

Helpline: 0808 800 2222
Textphone: 0800 783 6783
Fax: 020 7284 5501
e-mail: centraloffice@parentlineplus.org.uk
Website: www.parentlineplus.org.uk

Provides a freephone helpline called Parentline and courses for parents via the Parent Network Service. Parentline Plus also includes the National Stepfamily Association. For all information, call the Parentline freephone number: 0808 800 2222.

Parents Advice Centre
Floor 4, Franklin House
12 Brunswick Street
Belfast BT2 7GE

Helpline: 028 9023 8800
Tel: 028 9031 0891
Fax: 028 9031 2475
e-mail: belfast@pachelp.org
Website: www.pachelp.org

A voluntary organisation that offers support, guidance and counselling to parents and young people with family difficulties.

Parents at Work
45 Beech Street
London EC2Y 8AD

Tel: 020 7628 3565
Fax: 020 7628 3591
e-mail: info@parentsatwork.org.uk
Website: www.parentsatwork.org.uk

Provides advice and information about childcare provision.

Positive Parenting
1st Floor
2A South Street
Gosport PO12 1ES

Tel: 023 9252 8787
Fax: 023 9250 1111
e-mail: info@parenting.org.uk
Website: www.parenting.org.uk

Aims to prepare people for the role of parenting by helping parents, those about to become parents and also those who lead parenting groups.

raisingkids.co.uk
Website: www.raisingkids.co.uk

This website provides Individual advice from Dr Pat Spungin and other qualified experts, a huge reference library of parenting solutions, plus online discussions for support from the raisingkids. co.uk online community of parents in similar situations.

Relate
Herbert Gray College
Little Church Street
Rugby CV21 3AP
Tel: 01788 573 241
e-mail: enquiries@national.relate.org.uk
Website: www.relate.org.uk

In Northern Ireland:
76 Dublin Road
Belfast BT2 7HP
Tel: 028 9032 3454

Provides a confidential counselling service for relationship problems of any kind. Local branches are listed in the phone book.

Twins and Multiple Birth Association (TAMBA)
2 The Willows
Gardner Road
Guildford
Surrey GU1 4PG

Helpline 01732 868000 (Mon–Fri 7–11 p.m.; weekends 10 a.m.–
   11 p.m.)
Tel: 0870 770 3305
Fax: 0870 770 3303
e-mail: enquiries@tamba.org.uk
Website: www.tamba.org.uk

Gives information and support to families with twins, triplets and more.

Parenting Courses

Parentalk Parenting Course

A new parenting course designed to give parents the opportunity to share their experiences, learn from each other and discover some principles of parenting. For more information, phone 020 7450 9073.

Positive Parenting

Publishes a range of low-cost, easy-to-read, common-sense resource materials that provide help, information and advice. Responsible for running a range of parenting courses across the UK. For more information, phone 023 9252 8787.

Parent Network

For more information, call Parentline Plus on 0808 800 2222.

More About Paren**T**alk

Launched in 1999, in response to research which revealed that 1 in 3 parents feel like failures, Parentalk is all about inspiring parents to make the most of their vitally important role.

A registered charity, we exist to provide relevant information and advice for mums and dads in a format that they feel most comfortable with, regardless of their background or family circumstances.

Our current activities include:

- **The Parentalk Parenting Principles Course**
  Already used by almost 25,000 mums and dads, this video-based resource brings together groups of parents to share their experiences, laugh together and learn from one another. Filmed at the studios of GMTV, endorsed by the National Confederation of Parent Teacher Associations and featuring Parentalk Founder Steve Chalke, the course is suitable for use by groups of parents in their own homes or by schools, PTAs, pre-schools and nurseries, health visitors, health centres, family centres, employers, churches and other community groups.

- **Parentalk Local Events**
  Looking at every age group from the toddler to the teenage years, and from how to succeed as a parent to how to succeed as a grandparent, Parentalk evenings are a specially tailored, fun mixture of information, shared stories and advice for success as a mum, dad or grandparent. Operating across the country, the Parentalk team of speakers can also provide input on a range of more specialist subjects such as helping

your child sleep or striking a healthy balance between work and family life.

- **Parentalk at Work Events**

  Parentalk offer lunchtime and half-day workshops for employers and employees, at their place of work, that look at getting the balance right between the responsibilities of work and those of a family. Parentalk also provides a life coaching service for employees, helping them to deal with the pressures they encounter at home in order to be happier, and perform better, at work.

  All Parentalk at Work initiatives are backed up by a comprehensive website: **www.parentalk.co.uk/atwork**

- **The Parentalk Guide Series**

  In addition to the 'How to Succeed' series, Parentalk offers a comprehensive series of titles that look at a wide variety of parenting issues. All of these books are easy-to-read, down-to-earth and full of practical information and advice.

- **The Parentalk Schools Pack**

  This resource, designed especially for year 9 pupils, builds on the success of the Parentalk Video Course, to provide material for eight lessons on subjects surrounding preparing for parenthood. The pack has been tailored to dovetail with the PHSE and citizenship curriculum and is available for teachers to download from the Parentalk website.

- **www.parentalk.co.uk**

  www.parentalk.co.uk is a lively, upbeat site exclusively for parents, packed with fun ideas, practical advice and some great tips for making the most of being a mum or dad.

To find out more about any of these Parentalk initiatives or our plans for the future, or to receive our

quarterly newsletter, contact a member of the team at the address below:

Parentalk
115 Southwark Bridge Road
London SE1 0AX
Tel: 020 7450 9073
Fax: 020 7450 9060
e-mail: info@parentalk.co.uk

**Helping parents make the most of every stage
of their child's growing up.**

(Registered Charity No: 1074790)